AFRICAN AMERICAN COLLECTION

DISTRICT OF COLUMBIA

Runaway and Fugitive Slave Cases

1848–1863

District of Columbia
Department of Corrections
Runaway Slave Book
1848–1863

United States District Court
for the District of Columbia
Fugitive Slave Cases
1862–1863

Jerry M. Hynson

HERITAGE BOOKS
2012

HERITAGE BOOKS

AN IMPRINT OF HERITAGE BOOKS, INC.

Books, CDs, and more—Worldwide

For our listing of thousands of titles see our website
at
www.HeritageBooks.com

Published 2012 by
HERITAGE BOOKS, INC.
Publishing Division
100 Railroad Ave. #104
Westminster, Maryland 21157

International Standard Book Numbers
Paperbound: 978-1-58549-069-1
Clothbound: 978-0-7884-9381-2

Table of Contents

INTRODUCTION

The Fugitive Slave Law of 1850 required that the alleged owner of a fugitive slave prove ownership before a federal commissioner [1]. Proof of ownership could be in one of two forms, an affidavit from the court of a slave state or, by the testimony of white witnesses. If the commissioner decided against the claimant, he, the commissioner, received a fee of five dollars, if in favor, ten dollars. The fee increase was justified by the increase in paper work required in returning the fugitive to the slave state.

U.S. marshals and deputies were required to assist slaveowners in capturing their property. They were fined one thousand dollars if they refused to assist. Marshals were empowered to deputize citizens on the spot to aid in seizing a fugitive. Stiff criminal penalties were imposed on citizens harboring fugitives or obstructing their capture.

The agency responsible for the administration and enforcement of the law in the District of Columbia The U. S. Circuit Court for the District of Columbia. The performance of these duties generated a series of records relating to manumissions, emancipations, and claims of owners of fugitive slaves. These records contain references to owners, location of slaves, relationships between slaves, and other personal data. Original records are maintained at the National Archives in Washington, D. C, as a part of Record Group 21.[2] In the abstracts contained in this volume, an attempt has been made to provide the user with sufficient information to encourage further research. For the most part the abstracts include the name of the slave or slaves, the name and home county of the alleged owner or claimant, and the date of the court action. It should be noted that where a county is indicated, that county is located in Maryland.

The capture of a fugitive slave required the availability to house that slave until the action of the court could be completed. In the District of Columbia, slaves were housed in what has been called "the D. C. Slave Jail." The records of the slave jail provide references to slave owners and

---

[1] A new office created by the law.

[2] *Records of the United States District Court for the District of Columbia Relating to Slaves. 1851-1863* (National Archives Microfilm Publication M433, 3 rolls), RG 21, NACP, Roll # 3.

persons responsible for the committing of the slave to the slave jail. Such persons were often owners utilizing the facilities of the jail to house their slaves while they attended to business in the District of Columbia. On other occasions they were agents of the owners who, having apprehended the slaves, housed them in the jail while awaiting court action. The release of a slave to the custody of person often indicates an owner, an owner's agent, or a relative of the slave. The latter case was applicable when an alleged slave was proven to be free.

Microfilm publication of this record is available at the Maryland State Archives, Annapolis, Md. [3]

---

[3] *D. C. Department of Corrections Runaway Slave Book* (Maryland State Archives Microfilm Publication M9597, 1 roll), Special Collections, Maryland State Archives.

1848 – 1863
D. C. Department of Corrections
Runaway Slave Book

John Calvert: Committed by order of H. C. Williams 6 April 1848. Released 22 June 1848 to William H. Williams.

Isaiah Lemmons: Committed by order of James Marshall 23 May 1848. Released 29 June 1848. Free man.

Margaret: Committed by order of B. H. Worrell 28 May 1848. Discharged 16 November 1848 to B. O. Sheckells.

Charlotte: Committed 22 June 1848 upon by order of J. Marshall & Thomas A. Hawks. Released 5 July 1848 to L. F. Bowie.

H. Hemsley: Committed 23 June 1848 upon by order of W. T. Mitchell. Released 28 June 1848 to J. T. Vantyre.

Israel: Committed 24 June 1848 upon by order of William Beach. Released 25 June 1848 to Mrs. Rhodes.

Tom: Committed 28 June 1848 by order of J. S. Buckley. Released 5 July 1848 to M. B. Bruton.

Elizabeth Addison and two children: Committed 5 July 1848. Released to Z. B. Bell 22 July 1848.

Ann Johnson: Committed 6 July 1848. Released to Dr. Bond 18 September 1848.

Harriett Hemsley: Committed 6 July 1848. Released

6 September 1848 to Mrs. McCor____.

Mary and child: Committed 12 July 1848. Upon by order of A. Redbird. Released 7 September 1848 to S. Sheriff.

Charles: Committed 15 July 1848 upon by order of J. Dove. Released 11 September 1848 to Lin. Osborne.

Richard Chisley: Committed 18 July 1848 upon by order of R. R. Binn. Released 12 September 1848 to James Naylor.

Hester: Committed 22 July 1848 upon by order of R. R. Binn. Released 18 September 1848 to W. E. F. Bernard.

Osea Partes: Committed 1 August 1848 upon by order of William Anderson. Released 27 September 1848 to Dr. Breaves.

William Harrison: Committed 4 August 1848. Released 27 September 1848 to William Maryman.

George Parker & James Stewart: Committed 19 August 1848 by order of William A. Malloy. Released to Otho Bell 27 September 1848

Ben: Committed 19 August 1848 by order of L. A. Released 3 October 1848 to John Little.

Sarah Ann: Committed 23 August 1848 by order of William

Morgan. Released 3 October 1848 to H. C. Mathews.

Salina: Committed 24 August 1848 by order of Hanson Brown. Released 26 September 1848 to Mr. Brown.

Benjamin Bell: Committed 5 October 1848 by order of F. B. Poston. Released 13 October 1848 to J. P. Gosman.

Judson Brooks: Committed 8 October 1848 by order of William A. Malloy. Released 15 October to John ___.

Charles: Committed 8 October 1848 by order of William A. Malloy. Released 9 October 1848 to J. W. Beck.

George Wilson: Committed 8 October 1848 by order of W. Sanderson. Released 15 October to John Bessey.

Billy Sprigg: Committed 14 October 1848 by order of William Morgan Released to Judson Clarke 20 October 1848.

Mary Ann: Committed 18 October 1848 by Thomas Plumsett for "safekeeping". Released 28 October 1848 to C. Alexander.

John Overhall: Committed 23 October 1848. Released 1 November to V. N. Glass___.

Samuel: Committed 24 October 1848 by order of J. S. Brickley. Released 26 October 1848 to J. M. Parkin

John Gasttridge: Committed 30 October 1848 by order of J. R. Minor. Released 16 November 1848 to William ___.

Jane & her child: Committed 30 October 1848 by order of

R. Shaw. Released 3 November to James ,Garrison .

Arianna: Committed 4 November 1848 by order of John H. Selby. Released 16 November to Amos Bell.

Beverly Jackson: Committed 7 November 1848 by order of James Brown. Released to Isaac M___ 30 November 1848.

Washington: Committed 13 November by order of Henry Hawes for 'safekeeping'. Released 16 January 1849 to George Richards.

Bob Scott: Committed 13 November 1848 by order of John N. Goddard and William Morgan Released by order of John N. Goddard to Thomas W. Ceagall/Segal. 21 November 1848.

Levy/Levi Diggs: Committed 14 November 1848 by order of Wilson Dove for George Rhodes for 'safekeeping'. Released 16 December 1848 by order of George Rhodes to G. W. Earhardt.

Sarah Ann: Committed 15 November 1848 by order of J. B. Magruder for William Barton. Released 21 November 1848 to J. B. Magruder.

Henry: Committed 16 November 1848 by order of James Crandell for William Sanderson. Released 18 November 1848 to F. Monroe by order of James Crandell.

Ben Harris: Committed 21 November 1848 by J. N. Goddard for William Morgan Released 28 November 1848 to

William B. P. Coop, overseer by order of John H. Goddard.

Ellen Linsey/Livsey: Committed 21 November 1848 by James Crandell for John L. Fowler. . **Found to be Free.** Released 22 November by order of James Crandell.

Jane Davis: Committed by T. C. Davis 22 November 1848 as a runaway. Released 15 January 1849 .

Bennett: Committed 1 December 1848 as a runaway. Released To George Diggs 1 January 1849.

Hatim: Committed 6 December 1848 by C. Woodward for safekeeping. Released to Dr. 8 January 1849.

Alfred: Committed 8 December 1848 by T. C. Donn as a Runaway. Released 8 January 1849 to Henry Brooke.

George: Committed 13 December 1848 by James Crandell as a runaway. Released to J. R. Missos 12 January 1849.

Henny: Committed 17 December 1848 by James Crandell as a runaway. Released 31 January to J. R. Minor.

Hinny: Committed 18 December 1848 by T. C. Donn Released to W. W. Gale 5 February 1849.

Tom: Committed 27 December 1848 by J. Crandell as a runaway. Released 16 January 1849 to T. R. Brooks.

Sam: Committed 3 January 1849 by James Crandell and J. S. Brickley as a runaway. Released 5 February 1849. To J. S. Thorn

Mary: Committed 11 February 1849 by James Crandell and H. Vermillion as a runaway from

Millikin (possible surname of owner ?). Released 13 February 1849 to George Thompson. (possible manager or overseer for Millikin).

Osse Wood: Committed 13 February by John H. Goddard and O. E. P. Hazard as a runaway from D. Baldwin. Released to William Watson 19 February 1849.

Sarah King: Committed 14 February by Theodore F. Bowie for C. L. Gantt for safekeeping. Released 16 February 1849 to William H. Barton.

Charlotte: Committed 24 February 1849 by James Brown for H. Trunnell for safekeeping . Release 19 March to H. Trunnell.

Oswald Wood: Committed 1 March 1849 by John D. Bowling and Charles McDonald as a runaway. Released to John D. Bowling 13 March 1849.

Robert Brown: Committed 2 March 1849 by John H. Goddard and R. Waters as a Runaway from Clagett. Released to Smith Thompson 19 March 1849.

Washington: Committed 2 March 1849 by James L. Smith as a runaway. Released to R. T. McGill.

George Tinker: Committed 5 March 1849 by Thomas Ball as a runaway. Released 9 March 1849 to Robert Bowie of Walter.

George Brooke: Committed 7 March 1849 by William Morgan as a runaway. Released to John W. Mudd for Dominik Mudd 19 March 1849.

Clarissa Carrol: Committed 10 March 1849 by Henry Robinson as a runaway. Released 19 March 1849 to Reuben Simmons.

Phillip Bruce: Committed 12 March 1849 by James G. Webb for safekeeping. Released to James Allen 18 March 1849.

Julia Swann: Committed 13 March 1849 by John R. Minor as a runaway. Released 23 March 1849 to John Adams.

Barney Ellis: Committed 14 March 1849 as a runaway by Robert Waters. Released 19 March 1849 to William B. Cross.

Lucretia: Committed 20 March 1849 by Hendrick & Harney. Released 23 March to Edna W. Duvall.

George Montgomery: Committed 30 March 1849 for safekeeping. Released 12 April 1849 to J. B___.

Ann Johnson: Committed 4 April 1849 by Ignatius Howe as a runaway. Released 17 April 1849 to J. Dyer/Dryer.

Hezekiah Evans: Committed 10 April 1849 as runaway. Proven free and released 21 April 1849.

Winney Cayes & Turner Cayes: Committed 12 April 1849 by James Cocke for safekeeping. Released 17 April 1849 and 24 April 1849 respectively to H. B. Robertson.

Frank and Stephen: Committed 12 April 1849 by A Hoover for safekeeping. Release data is illegible.

Harriet A. Taylor: Committed 13 April 1849 as a runaway by John Wheaton. Released 17 April 1849 to William J. Thomas.

John Brook: Committed 15 April 1849 by John R. Minor as a runaway. Released 25 April 1849 to William F. Gassaway .

William Hall: Committed 15 April 1849 by John Adams as a runaway. Released 18 April 1849 to John A. Harrison.

Bailey Beall: Committed 15 April 1849 by John Adams as a runaway. Released 18 April 1849 to E. P. Legg.

William: Committed 16 April 1849 by Richard Brookings for safekeeping. Released 17 April 1849 to James L. Gray.

Humphrey: Committed 16 April by R. W. Waters as a runaway from ___ Belt. Released 25 April 1849 to A. C. Belt.

Chloe Hodges: Committed 19 April 1849 by J. F. Wollard as a runaway. Released 28 April 1849 to Mrs. Holmes

Harry: Committed 20 April 1849 by James Gates as a runaway. Released 22 May to John H. Nelson.

Henry Lee: Committed 23 April 1849 as a runaway by J. W. Kitchens. Released as free 25 April 1849.

Humphrey: Committed 26 April 1849 for safekeeping. Release not recorded.

Tyler: Committed 26 April 1849 by Theodore A. Hanks as a runaway from ___ Bell. Released to Z. Bell 1 May 1849.

Alfred Martin: Committed 28 April 1849 by Gustavius White for safekeeping. Released 2 May 1849 to Mrs. Simpson.

Richard: Committed 29 April 1849 by John R. Mann as a runaway. Released 30 April to B. J. Semmes

Patrick and Cato: Committed 2 May 1849 as runaways by William Morgan Released 7 May 1849 to Henry Weaver.

Warner; Committed 5 May 1849 by W. C. Fairfax for safekeeping. Released to his mother 15 May 1849.

Edward Brooks: Committed 10 May 1849 by Dew___ and Hilton as a runaway. No release notes.

Jacob, Isabella, Lucy and Vina: Committed 15 April 1849 for safekeeping. Released to B. O. Sheckells 16 May 1849.

Catherine: Committed 20 May 1849 by Joseph Shepherd as a runaway. Released 22 May to Thomas H. Edelon.

Jefferson: Committed 21 May 1849 for safekeeping. Released 25 May 1849 to William H. Williams.

Maranda: Committed 24 May 1849 by Ann E. Beal for safekeeping. Released 2 June 1849 to John E. Petlow.

Boy Clevis: Committed 26 May 1849 by James Simpson as a runaway. Released 2 June 1849 to B. Beall.

Lewis: Committed 27 May 1849 for safekeeping . Released 31 May to William Morgan

James: Committed 30 May 1849 as runaway from ___ Ball.

Released 3 June 1849 to O. B. Ball.

Charles: Committed 31 May 1849 by R. Waters as a runaway. Released 5 June 1849 to *illegible name.*

Pleasant: Committed 3 June 1849 by John Adams as a runaway. Released 15 June 1849 to John F. Newman.

Charles Edelin: Committed 5 June 1849 by John Smith as a runaway. Released 7 June 1849 to *illegible name.*

Susan Sheavers alias Susannah Safes: Committed 10 June 1849 by William Cox as a runaway. Released as free 12 June 1849.

Ritta and Jerry: Committed 12 June 1849 Edward L. Darcey for safekeeping. Released 12 June 1849 to Edward L. Darcey.

Thomas: Committed 15 June 1849 by John R. Minor as a runaway. Released on 19 June 1849 to E. M. Linthicum.

Nat: Committed 18 June 1849 as a runaway by A. Fleming. Released 21 June 1849 to William Duvall.

Grace: Committed 23 June 1849 by Phillip R. Fendall for safekeeping. Released to George T. Richards.

Kitty Freaser: Committed 25 June 1849 as a runaway by R. H. Clements. Released to Blanford.

Frederick: Committed 25 June 1849 by John Adams. No release noted.

Sam: Committed 25 June 1849 as a runaway by J. W. Beck. Released 26 June 1849 to B. O. Sheckells.

Edward Chase: Committed 27 June 1849 as a runaway by John Adams. Released to F. N. Botcher, agent for the state of Maryland 14 November 1849.

Frederick: Committed 9 May 1849 by John Adams as a runaway. Released to E. Y. Harding 30 June 1849.

Edward Brooke: Committed 11 May 1849 by John Dewdney. . Released 16 April 1849 on writ of habeas corpus from Kent Circuit Court.

John Atkins: Committed 3 July 1849 as a runaway by Anthony Gray. Released Released 4 July 1849 to John __ Jenkins.

Gustavius: Committed 3 July 1849 by Robert Mills as a runaway. Released 10 July 1849 to Thomas H. Soltleford.

Charles Beans: Committed 4 July 1849 by John S. Fowler as a runaway. Released 10 July 1849 to _____ Coop.

Rachel: Committed 5 July 1849 by H. Safborough for safekeeping. Released 16 July 1849 to Jesse Griffin.

Sarah: Committed 5 July 1849 by R. H. Speake for safekeeping. Released 9 July 1849 to William H. Williams.

John Brook: Commited 6 July 1849 by Hanson Brown as a runaway. Released to John H. Payton.

George: Committed 7 July 1849 by William Morgan Jr. as a runaway. Released 9 July 1849 to John H. Sewalt.

Charles: Committed 9 July 1849 by William H. Willison for safekeeping. Released 19 July 1849 to William A. G____ .

Townley: Committed 14 July 1849 by Robert T. Mills as a runaway belonging to _____ Chew. Released 14 July 1849 to G. G. Harris.

Eliza Williams: committed 14 July 1849 by R. R. Bun as a runaway. Released 11 August 1849 to George T. Richards. Was delivered of a female child 17 July by Dr. Mather & Jones

Charles Stepney: Committed 17 July 1849 by Thomas Wilson for safekeeping. Released 27 September 1849 to Thomas Wilson.

Susan: Committed 21 July 1849 for safekeeping by Lloyd L. Beale. Released 22 July 1849 to L. L. Beale.

Tom: Committed 11 July 1849 by J. W. Wright as a runaway. Released 25 July 1849 to Margaret Fidden.

Charlotte and Julian: Committed 23 July 1849 as runaways. Released 24 July 1849 to Zachariah Shaw.

Robert: Committed 23 July 1849 by William H. Pagett as a runaway. Released 30 August 1849 to A. Smith.

James Thomas: Committed 23 July 1849 as a runaway from Duvall by Thomas Ball. Released 25 July 1849 by William Duvall.

Rachel: Committed 27 July 1849 by John Adams for safekeeping. Released 27 August to ____ Johnson.

John Thomas: Committed 27 July 1849 by John Adams for safekeeping. Released to Johnson.

Robert: Committed 28 July 1849 by John Adams for safekeeping. Released to Johnson.

John Doston. Committed 31 July 1849 by William F. Mackey as a runaway. Released 2 August 1849 as free to William H. Russell.

Charity: committed 6 August 1849 by William Morgan Jr. as a runaway from Pumphrey. Released 7 August 1849 to John Cook.

George Washington: Committed 7 August 1849 by by James S. Buckley as a runaway from Brooks. Released 22 September 1849 to Joseph Brenner.

Robert alias Jacob: Committed 9 August 1849 by Robert T. Mills as runaway from Roberts. Released 13 August 1849 to J. Ducket.

William Hussy: Committed 10 August 1849 as a runaway from Bowie by Hatch Cooke. Released 14 August 1849 to William H. Hall.

Julia: Committed 10 August 1849 by Piles L. Tolson as a runaway from Edlin. Released 19 August to John C. Cooke.

Henry Davis: Committed 13 August 1849 by A. Flemming for safekeeping for. Released 15 August 1849 to James H. Simpson.

Henry Tyler: Committed 18 August 1849 by James S. Buckley as a runaway. Released 19 August 1849 to John C. Cook.

Richard Fronike/: Committed 20 September 1849 by James Webster as a runaway from Wells. Released 6 September 1849 to J. B. Miller & W. W. Wathen

Susan Fronike/Fronille, Susan : Committed 20 September 1849 by James Webster as a runaway from Wells. Released 6 September 1849 to J. B. Miller & W. W. Wathen.

Eliza Mason and Child: Committed 3 September 1849 by R. R. Burr for safekeeping. Released 13 September 1849 to Joseph Brewer.

Henry Allen: Committed 7 September 1849 by H. T. L. Wilson as a runaway from Baden. Released 15 September 1849 to George T. Richards.

Nan Sewell: Committed 10 September 1849 by Raymond D. Klopfer as a runaway from Young. Released 12 September 1849 to George W. Young.

Hamish Brooke: Committed 10 September 1849 by Raymond D. Klopfer as a runaway from Bowie. Released 13 September 1849 to William H. Williams.

Charity: Committed by Edmund Gannan 10 September 1849 for safekeeping. Released September 1849 to Edmund Gannan.

Ameity: Committed by Edmund Gannan 10 September 1849 for safekeeping. Released September 1849 to Edmund Gannan.

Rachel Sewell: C14 September 1849 by F. B. Pastore for safekeeping. Released to Thomas H. Milburn 15 September 1849.

Jacob: Committed 15 September 1849 by James S. Buckley as a runaway. Released 23 September 1849 to George A. W. Turner.

Ned: Committed for safekeeping 17 September 1849. Released to William H. Richards 28 September 1849.

Jane: Committed 18 September 1849 by Edward Gannon for safekeeping. Released 25 September 1849 to Henry Bunch.

Edward: Committed 18 September 1849 by H. V. Hill for safekeeping. Released to William H. Williams 24 September 1849.

Clarra: Committed 19 September 1849 by Robert Wright for safekeeping. Released 22 September 1849 to Robert Wright.

James Henry Contee: Committed 21 September 1849 by R, H. Sedgewick as a runaway. Released 23 September 1849 to James H. Sampson.

James Queen: Committed 2 October 1849 by Thomas Jenkins for safekeeping. Released 3 October 1849 to B. O.Sheckells.

Edward: Committed 2 October 1849 by Samuel J. Beck for safekeeping. Released 3 October 1849 to Samuel J. Becky.

William: Committed 5 October 1849 by William Morgan Jr. as a runaway. Released 11 October 1849 to Rev. Joseph B. Lattimore.

Rode: Committed 7 October 1849 by Mary Ann Hall for safekeeping. Released 12 October 1849.

William: Committed 7 October 1849 by James G. Webster for safekeeping. Released 8 October 1849 to William H. Williams,

Joseph: Committed 7 October 1849 by James G. Webster for safekeeping. Released 8 October 1849 to William H. Williams.

John Henry: Committed 15 October 1849 for safekeeping by Edmond Gannon. Releases 25 October 1849 to Edmond Gannon.

Betsy & child: Committed 15 October 1849 by William Morgan Jr. as a runaway. Released to Elbert Perry.

Betsy & Child: Committed 17 October 1849 by Joseph Brown. Released to Elbert Perry.

Thomas: Committed 18 October 1849 by Harrison Wallis for safekeeping. Released 20 October 1849 to R. O. Sedgewick.

Emily: Committed 18 October 1849 by R. O. Sedgewick. Released 19 October 1849 to R. O. Sedgewick.

Henson: Committed 19 October 1849 by Allison Nailor for safekeeping. Released 20 October 1849 to John R. Fortwell.

George Lee: Committed 22 October 1849 by Milton W. Ward as a runaway. Released 23 October 1849 to Thomas Brown.

William Nicholls: Committed 26 October 1849 by Marshall

Browne for safekeeping.
Released 16 November 1849 to
William II. Williams.

George Wilson: Committed
31 October 1849 as a runaway
by John Shelton. Released 16
November 1849 to W. T.
Campbell.

Robert Hunter: Committed
4 November 1849 by Benjamin
Frazier as a runaway. Released
5 November to Joseph Brain.

Lewes: Committed 1 November
1849 by Anthony Gray as a
runaway. Released 3 November
to William B. Burnham.

Mary: Committed 3 November
1849 by E. G. Handy for
safekeeping. Released 1
December 1849.

Thomas Carroll: Committed
5 November 1849 by John
Davis as a runaway. Released 6
November 1849 to Lt. B. W.
Hunter.

James Jackson: Committed
6 November 1849by William
Morgan Jr. as a runaway.
Released 7 November 1849 to
William H. Williams.

Thomas: Committed 8 November
1849 by B. W. Hunter for
safekeeping. Released 11
December 1849 to B. W.
Hunter.

Jacob Gant: Committed
10 November 1849 by George
W. Walker for safekeeping.
Release 13 November 1849 to
George W. Walker.

Harriet Davis: Committed
10 November 1849 by R. R.
Burr as a runaway. Released 17
November 1849 to
William Beall.

Emily: committed 13 November
1849 by R. H. Sedgewick for
safekeeping. Released 16
November to William H.
Williams.

Martin Ransels: Committed
23 November 1849 by J. F.
Wollard and William H.
Barnstable as a runaway.
Released 26 November 1849 to
I. C. Chichister.

Samuel Smith: Committed
23 November 1849 by J. F.
Holland and William H.
Barnichols as a runaway.
Released 26 November 1849 to
William Richards.

Tompson R. Brooks: Committed
23 November 1849 by J. F.
Holland and William H.
Barnichols as a runaway.
Released 26 November 1849 to
Joseph Brian.

Charles Tailor: Committed
23 November 1849 by J. F.
Holland and William H.
Barnichols as a runaway.
Released 26 November 1849 to
Joseph Brian.

Alexander Jemmes: by J. F.
Holland and William H.
Barnichols as a runaway.
Released 26 November 1849 to
Joseph Brian.

Jacob Powell: by J. F. Holland and
William H. Barnichols as a
runaway. Released 26
November 1849 to Joseph
Brian.

Nansey: Committed 25 November
1849 by A. E. L. Kesse as a
runaway. Released 29
November 1849 to John H.
Calvin.

Jim: Committed 29 November
1849 by Phillip Ennis for

safekeeping. Released 30 November 1849 to Phillip Ennis.

Hannah: Committed 3 December 1949 for safekeeping by G. B. Hardes. Released 3 December 1849 to William H. Williams.

John W. Thomas: Committed 3 December 1849 by Bill Kloppers as a runaway from " Goodwin ". Released 3 December 1849 to H. B. Goodwin.

Mary: Committed 7 December 1849 for safekeeping. Released 11 December to Asbury.

George: Committed 10 December 1849 for safekeeping by John Adams. Released 11 December 1849 to William H. Williams.

Blaney Bingham: Committed 14 December 1849 by George W. Custas and John Adams for safekeeping. Released 27 December to William H. Williams.

Caroline Speaks: Committed 10 December 1849 by Henry Matthews for safekeeping. Released 11 December 1849 to William H. Williams.

Lucy Williams and child: Committed 16 December 1849 by E. G. Handy as a runaway. Released 19 December 1849 to J. H. C. Coffin.

Sarah Ann: Committed 16 December 1849 by David Westerfield as a runaway. Released 19 December 1849 to J. H. C. Coffin.

Louisa and Child: Committed 16 December 1849 David Westerfield as a runaway. Released 19 December 1849 to J. H. C. Coffin.

Emollient and Child: Committed 16 December 1849 David Westerfield as a runaway. Released 19 December 1849 to J. H. C. Coffin.

Thomas: Committed 26 December 1849 by B. W. Hunter for safekeeping. Released 28 December 1849 to Mrs. Hunter.

David: Committed 27 December 1849 Samuel W.Magruder for safekeeping. Released 5 January 1850 to William H. Williams.

William Lee: Committed 29 December 1849 by R. R. Bunn as a runaway. Released 1 January 1850 to John B. Hancocke.

Louisa Prim: Committed 7 January 1850 by E, G, Handy as a runaway. Released 1 February 1850 to _____ Cooke.

Lewis: Committed 12 January 1850 by Wallis Kirkwood for safekeeping. Released 12 January 1850 to Wallis Kirkwood.

John Snowden: Committed 14 January 1850 by M. W. Ward as a runaway. Released 17 January 1850 to T. P. Andrews and B. O. Sheckells.

Bob Browne: Committed 15 January 1850 by J. L. Buckley as runaway from "Jenkins". Released 17 January 1850 to Joseph I. Jenkins.

Henny: Committed 15 January 1850 by (name illegible) for safekeeping. Released 23 January 1850.

George Colbert: committed 19 January 1850 by John Davis

as a runaway. Released
23 January as a free man.
Earnest Neal: Committed
21 January 1850 by E. W.
Landsdale as a runaway.
Released 24 January 1850 to
William George Robertson and
William H. Williams.
Alice Taylor/Tyler: Committed
23 January 1850 by J. F.
Holland as a runaway. Released
29 January 1850 when proved
to be free
Matilda: Committed 29 January
1850 by William George
Robertson for safekeeping.
Released 20 January 1850 to
William H. Williams.
Isaac Thomas: Committed
27 January 1850 by Benjamin
Taylor as a runaway. Released
4 February 1850 to Matthew
Duvall.
Augustas: Committed 29 January
1850 by James Rhodes for
safekeeping. Released 15
February 1850 to William H.
Richards.
Cerena Masters: Committed
31 January 1850 by Theodore
Sheckeles as a runaway.
Released 11 February 1850 to
Arundel Smith.
Mimeo Downins: Committed
10 February 1850 James E. W.
Thompson as a runaway.
Released 11 February 1850 to
B. O. Sheckells.
William: Committed 10 February
1850 by William Bassie and
Samuel Bryan as a runaway.
Released 16 February 1850 J.
R. Inglehart and B. O.
Sheckells.
Solomon: Committed 10 February
1850 by William Bassie and

Samuel Bryan as a runaway.
Released 16 February 1850 to
J. R. Inglehart and B. O.
Sheckell.
Basil Hall: Committed 7 March
1850 by John Joy as a runaway.
Released 11 March 1850 to
H. W. Blunt and
James Williams.
Billy Butler: Committed 9 March
1850 by John Tomlin as a
runaway. Released 15 April
1850 having proved his
freedom.
William Shorter: Committed
12 March 1850 by R. R. ____
for safekeeping. Released 14
March 1850 to E. Fenwick.
Rosetta Hagen: Committed
12 March 1850 by C. L. Kess as
a runaway. Released 14 March
1850 to William H. Richards.
John Dinen: Committed 14 March
1850 by William A. Malloy as a
runaway. Released 23 April
1850 as free.
Henry Curtis: Committed
16 March 1850 by William H.
B____ as a runaway. Released
16 March to William Bind.
Frank Browne: Committed by
William Webster for
safekeeping. Released 5 May
1850 to John D. Bowling.
John T. Wood: Committed
21 March 1850 by James
Bowen as a runaway. Released
April 1850 to William B. Jones.
William: Committed 28 March
1850 by ____ for safekeeping.
Released 7 April 1850.
Sam: Committed 30 March 1850
by David Westerfield as a
runaway. Released 9 April 1850
upon proving himself free.

John Matthews: Committed 30 March 1850 as a runaway. Released 31 march 1850 having proven his freedom.

Jim: Committed 31 March 1850 by _____ Lanham for safekeeping. Released 1 April 1850 to _____ Lanham.

William: Committed 1 April 1850 by M. M. Wards as a runaway. Released 4 April 1850 to ____.

Sandy Hynson: Committed 2 April 1850 by Rezin Pumphrey as a runaway. Released 11 April 1850 to _____ Robinson.

Cary Ann: Committed 3 April 1850 by James Bowen as a runaway. Released 11 April 1850 to G. A. Duvall.

Martin Bradford: Committed 11 April 1850 as a runaway. Released 5 June 1850 to Robert H. Lewis.

William: Committed 28 March 1850 for safekeeping by Jackson Pierce. Released 7 April 1850 to Jackson Pierce.

Sam: Committed 30 March 1850 by David Westerfield as a runaway. Released 9 April 1850 having proven himself free.

John Matthews: Committed 30 March 1850 by Martin Cox as a runaway. Released 11 April. Freedom proved by H. s.

Jim: Committed 31 March for safekeeping by Thomas (illegible). Released 20 April 1850.

William: Committed 1 April 1850 M. M. Warde as a runaway. Released 4 April 1850 to A. Graves.

Sandy Henson: Committed 2 April 1850 by Rezen Pumphrey as a

runaway. Released 11 April to _____ Robinson.

Cary Ann: Committed 3 April 1850 by James Bowen as a runaway. Released 11 April 1850 to G. A. Duvall.

Martin Bradford: Committed 4 April 1850 by Alex McCarslow as a runaway. Released 5 June 1850 to Robert H. Lewis.

John Pecke: Committed 8 April 1850 by Seth Hyatt for safekeeping. Released 15 April 1850 to Seth Hyatt.

____ Anderson: Committed 11 April 1850 by A. E. L. Reese as a runaway. Released 12 April 1850 to Jonathon McGarrity.

Margaret: Committed 15 April 1850 by James S. Buckley as a runaway. Released 15 April 1850 to William H. Williams.

Mary: Committed 20 April 1850 by James Bowen as a runaway. Release 20 June 1850 to B. O. Sheckells.

S__ Sales and child: Committed 20 April 1850 by John Majors as a runaway. Released 22 April 1850 as free.

John Thomas Samson: Committed 22 April 1850 by J. C. Mitcherson for safekeeping. Released 28 April 1850 to William H. Williams.

Joseph Brooks: Committed 22 April 1850 by Major William B. Scott for safekeeping. Released 22 May 1850 to George T. Richards.

Henry: Committed 24 April 1850by Robert Mills as a runaway. Released 24 April 1850 to E. Magruder.

Henry Brooks: Committed 30 April 1850 by John Adams as a runaway. Released 4 May 1850 to John Parsons.

Henry Johnson: Committed 19 May 1850 by John Adams as a runaway. Released 4 June 1850 to John Parsons.

Henny: Committed 21 May 1850 by Edward Birdhead as a runaway. Released 21 May 1850 to Edward Horne.

George: Committed 22 May 1850 by John Kelly as a runaway. Released 24 May 1850 to Henry Harding.

Priscilla Gray: Committed 10 June 1850 by William Webster as a runaway. Released 11 June to William E. Pumphrey.

Cealia Stewart alias Cecilia Clarke: Committed 13 June 1850 by I, M,. Busher as a runaway. Released after proving her freedom. Date not noted.

Jane Davis and infant child: Committed 13 June 1850 by John B. Stanskiny as a runaway. Released 18 June 1850 to Walter A. Coles.

Edward Russell: Committed 14 June 1850 by ____ Ward as a runaway. Released 22 June to F. Redville.

Sally: Committed 15 June 1850 for safekeeping by J. M. Bucher. Released 17 June 1850 to J. M. Bucher.

Joe: Committed 10 June 1850 as a runaway by J. M. Bucher. Released 1 July 1850 to William _____.

Jane: Committed 17 June 1850 by James Bowen as a runaway.

Released 18 June 1850 to John H. G. McGruder.

Mims Louise: Committed 26 June 1850 by James W. Busher for safekeeping. Released 20 June 1850 to James W. McGinis.

Barbara Duckeston: Committed 29 June 1850 by J. M. Wright as a runaway. Released 12 July 1850 to Thomas Boothes/Brooks.

Maria Bowie: Committed 3 July 1850 as a runaway by Jobe Wright. Released 5 July 1850 to Samuel Carroll.

Matilda: Committed 10 July 1850 for safekeeping by Franklin Waters. Released 11 July 1850 to Franklin Waters,

George Badecourt: Committed 9 July 1850 as a runaway by H. G. H. Wilson . Released 15 July 1850 having been proven free.

Vachel: Committed 17 July 1850 as a runaway by Thomas Wright. Released 5 August 1850 to William H. Bowie.

Milly: Committed 19 July 1850 by J. Martin for safekeeping. Released 25 July 1850 to William H. Williams.

Hilliary Johnson: Committed 25 July 1850 by John Adams as a runaway. Released 26 July 1850 to James W. Claggett.

Jerry: Committed 27 July 1850 by W. W. Ward as a runaway. Released 29 July to William H. Williams.

Sandy: Committed 27 July 1850 by W. W. Ward as a runaway. Released 29 July to William H. Williams.

Ned Jones: Committed 28 July 1850 by R. R. Dunn (Bunn ?) as a runaway. Released 1 August 1850 to William Corts.

Hannah West & child: Committed 30 July 1850 by John Adams as a runaway. Released 1 August 1850 to Walter Carroll.

Delilia: Committed 30 July 1850 as a runaway by James Bowen. Released 19 August 1850 to Samuel B. Hall and William H. Richards.

Jim: Committed 30 July 1850 by James Bowen for safekeeping. Released 30 July 1850 to J. C. Cook.

Margery: Committed 2 August 1850 by Thomas J. Britts as a runaway. Released 3 August 1850 to Samuel Sprigg.

Anthony Garrett (Garnett ?): Committed 11 August 1850 by William Davidson as a runaway. Released 15 August 1850 to John A. & Fanny Lee.

Dennis Watkins: Committed 6 August 1850 by J. M. Buskin as a runaway. Released 9 August 1850 when proven free.

Mary Jones: Committed 9 August 1850 by J. H. Goddard as a runaway . Released 15 August 1850 to Henry Harding.

Allen: committed 10 August 1850 by E. G. Handy as a runaway. Released 12 August 1850 to J. C. Cook

Henry Thomas: Committed 10 August 1850 by H. C. Williams as a runaway. Released 10 August 1850 to S. S. Wilson.

John Woods: Committed 11 August 1850 by R. R. Bass as a runaway. Released 11 August to Horne & Gannon.

Henny Woods: Committed 11 August 1850 by R. R. Bass as a runaway. Released 11 August to Horne & Gannon.

Is___: Committed 11 August 1850 as a runaway by R. R. Bass. Released 14 August 1850 to Oden Bowie.

B___: Committed 12 August 1850 by J. F. Wollard as a runaway. Released 4 September 1850 to B. Thomas.

Matthew: Committed 12 August 1850 by William Corse as a runaway. Released 4 September 1850 to B. Thomas.

Dolly: Committed 13 August 1850 as a runaway by James Bowen. Released 4 September 1850 to R. O. Mulliken.

Serena: Committed 22 August 1850 by James Bowen as a runaway. Releases 23 August 1850 to A. Smith.

Margaret, Margaret T., & James Lewis: Committed 27 August 1850 by J. M. Carlile for safekeeping. Released 31 August to James Lewis.

Azaline Chase alias Winters: Committed 29 August 1850 by John Morgan as a runaway. Released 2 September 1850 having proven her freedom.

Richard Countes/Countee: Committed 29 August 1850 by John Morgan as a runaway. Released 121 September having proven his freedom.

Eliza & child: Committed 6 September 1850 by William H. Bland for safekeeping. Released 9 September 1850 to William H. Bland.

Jane Slater/Staten: Committed 15 September 11850 by R. R.

Bass as a runaway. Released
15 September 1850 to Thomas
Bassy & Joseph Fro_.
Betsy: Committed 16 September
1850 by Robert White as a
runaway. Released 15 October
1850 to _. Brooks & Robert P.
Wade.
Harriet: Committed 19 September
1850 by James Bowen as a
runaway. Released 25
September 1850 to Sam
Phillips.
Jacob: Committed 21 September
1850 by William H. Richards
for safekeeping. Released (date
illegible) to William
H.Richards.
Richard: Committed 24 September
1850 by Thomas Jackson for
safekeeping. Released 1
October 1850 to Thomas
Jackson.
Amelia: Committed 25 September
1850 by B. D. Kloffen
(Klossen ?) as a runaway.
Released 1 October to
M.H. Letton.
James/Jane Smith: Committed
26 September 1850 by William
A. Malloy as a runaway.
Released 5 October 1850 to
John H. Marbury.
Washington: Committed
27 September 1850 by
John Adams for safekeeping.
Released to B. O. Sheckells 30
September 1850.
James Jones: Committed
28 September 1850 by Wilson
Davis as a runaway. Released 5
October 1850 to Joshua Long.
Henrietta: Committed 1 October
1850 by John Adams for
safekeeping. Released 11
November 1850 ____ Disen.

Thomas: Committed 1 October
1850 by William H Bar___ for
safekeeping. Released 13
November 1850 to William H.
Williams.
Henny & 2 children: Committed
2 October 1850 by William A.
Mullay as runaways. Released
to A. A. Callis & George
Richards.
Dolly Johnson: Committed
4 October 1850 by William A.
Mullay as a runaway. Released
7 October 1850 to B. O.
Sheckells.
John Edwards: Committed
12 October 1850 by William
Martin as a runaway.
Apparently deceased while in
custody. Released to J. S. Erick.
Molly Hampkins: committed
12 October 1850 by William
Wheat as a runaway. Released
15 October 1850 to
Fenten M. Fitzhugh.
Rachail (Rachel ?): Committed
16 October 1850 by Martin M.
Ward as a runaway. Released
19 October 1850 to B. Mackall.
Frank: Committed 17 October
1850 by M. W. Ward as a
runaway. Releases 11
November 1850 to Thomas
Ward.
George Diggs: Committed
18 October 1850 by James A.
Payne as runaway. Released
19 October 1850 to
William. Offick.
Letty: Committed 19 October 1850
by B. D. Klapfin as a runaway.
Released 19 October 1850 to
H. Cooke.
James Williams: Committed
19 October 1850 by William A.

Malloy as a runaway. Released 28 October 1850 to _____.

Sarah: Committed 21 October 1850 by Frances Quigley for safekeeping. Released 28 October 1850 to Frances Quigley.

Henry Hubbard: Committed 21 October 1850 by Thomas Hunter as a runaway. Released 15 November 1850 to William Brewer and John S. Payton

William Dougherty: Committed 21 October 1850 by W. M. Ward as a runaway. Released 25 October 1850 to H. Cooke.

Margaret Green: Committed 26 October 1850 by James Simpson as a runaway. Released 30 October 1850 to John H. Dixon.

Harry Dune: Committed 28 October 1850 by Morton W. Ward as a runaway. Released 29 October 1850 to Alexander Keach Jr.,

Sam: Committed 30 October 1850 by James H. ___. As a runaway. Released 20 October 1850 to Thomas Jackson. [1]

Jeremiah Jennings: Committed 31 October 1850 as a runaway by Bradley ____. Released 4 November 1850 to Alexander Keach.

William Calvert: Committed 1 November 1850 by John E. Robey for safekeeping. Released 13 November 1850 to William H. Williams.

Joseph Molan: Committed 1 November 1850 by John E.

---

[1] Although this chronology does not make sense. This is what appears in the notebook.

Robey for safekeeping. Released 13 November 1850 to William H. Williams.

Ann & child: Committed 30 November 1850 by R. R. Burr for safekeeping. Released 11 November to Thomas Baldwin.

Isaac: Committed 3 November 1850 by R. W. Gordon as a runaway. Released 7 November 1850 to J. K. Roberts.

Peter: Committed 4 November 1850 by Thomas Caton as a runaway. Released 22 November 1850 to J. A. McLorten.

Stephen: Committed 4 November 1850 by G. W. B_____ for safekeeping. Released 13 November 1850 to William H. Williams.

John Bell: Committed 4 November 1850 by R. Y. Miles for safekeeping. Released 7 November 1850 to __ Manning.

Ben Campbell: Committed 6 November 1850 by O. E. P. Hazzard as a runaway. Released 11 November 1850 to John Goines.

Robert T. Tarter: Committed 6 November 1850 by James S. Buckley as a runaway. Released 26 November having proven his freedom.

Mary Ann: Committed 6 January 1851 by James Ennis for safekeeping. Released 7 January to Thomas B. Goddard.

Thomas Woods: Committed 8 January 1851 by B. Klopfus as a runaway. Released 13 January 1851 to John Kinsbury.

Mary: Committed 15 January 1851 by Joseph Lusby as a runaway.

Released 16 January 1851 to James G. Cadle.

Jess: Committed 17 January 1851 by James Byers as a runaway. Released 20 January 1851 to George F. Beatle.

Basil: Committed 20 January 1851 by B. D. Klopfer as a runaway. Released 25 January 1851 to William H. Guinn.

Basil: Committed 22 January 1851 by James S. Buckley as a runaway. Released 27 January to J. A. Osbourne.

Sena Brooks: Committed 23 January 1851 by H. Y. L. Wilson as a runaway. Released 25 January 1851 to Orsben Sprigg.

Parmars: Committed 27 January 1851 by John Trocke for safekeeping. Released 19 February 1851 to H. R. Maryman.

Richard Waters: Committed 18 February 1851 by E. G. Handy for safekeeping. Released 4 July 1851.

Nancy: Committed 24 February 1851 by E. G. Handy for safekeeping. Released 24 February to E. G. Handy.

John Butches: Committed 24 February 1851 for safekeeping by William Deans. Released 26 February to F. L. Leavens.

Emeline Jackson: Committed 15 March 1851 by E. G. Handy as a runaway. Released 19 March 1851 to Elbert _____

Louisa: Committed 14 March 1851 as a runaway by James H. Smith. Released 18 March 1851 to John Bowie.

Teresa Blackwell: Committed 22 March 1851 by A. E. L. Reese for safekeeping. Released 4 April 1851 to "self".

Tom: Committed 23 March 1851 by James Custer as a runaway. Releases 27 March 1851 to J. E. Q. Early.

Phillip Jackson: Committed 1 April 1851 by James Ennis as a runaway. Released 2 April 1851 to Thomas B. Goddard.

Alfred Shanks: Committed 4 April 1851 by William Case as a runaway. Released 7 April 1851 to Edwin C. Fitzhin.

Nace: Committed 4 April 1851 by A. E. L. Keese for safekeeping. Released 8 April 1851 to _____.

John: Committed 10 April 1851 by William Stone for safekeeping. Released 28 April 1851 to William Stone.

William: Committed 2_ April 1851 by James A. Bowen as a runaway. Released 2 May 1851 to Edward Hautt.

Milindia: Committed 27 April 1851 by Charles Scrivener for safekeeping. Released 28 April 1851 to "self".

Louisa: Committed between 27 April and 2 May 1851 by B. Washington for safekeeping. Released 28 April 1851 by order of B. Washington.

Charles Calvert: Committed 2 May 1851 by James S. Buckley as a runaway. Released 24 May 1851 to Charles R. Bealle.

Lerarge(LaGrange ?): Committed 3 May 1851 by Richard Southern for safekeeping.

Released 6 May 1851 to William Shreve.

John: Committed 6 May 1851 as a runaway by A. W. Marlow. Released 19 May 1851 to H. R. Harris & B. O. Schekells.

Jane: Committed 6 May 1851 as a runaway by A. W. Marlow. Released 19 May 1851 to A, B. Simms and J. C. Cook.

Townley: Committed 6 May 1851 by A. W. Marlow as a runaway. Released 13 May 1851 to J. H. Hawkins and J. C. Cooke.

Harriett: Committed 7 May 1851 by W. W. Heard as a runaway. Released 10 May 1851 to George Richards.

Robert Wilson: Committed 9 May 1851 by Jackson Morton for safekeeping. Released 12 May 1851 by order of Jackson Morton.

Lucinda: Committed 10 May 1851 by L. Harbaugh for safekeeping. Released 10 May 1851 to B. O. Sheckells.

Samuel: Committed 12 May 1851 by Ward/Wand as a runaway. Released 15 May 1851 to J. Warner.

Kitty Frazier: committed 12 May 1851 by William Duvall as a runaway. Released 17 May 1851 to D. R. Dyer.

Arthur: Committed 17 May 1851 by Thomas P. Ryon (Ryan?) as a runaway. Released 19 May 1851 to Benjamin Stockett.

Alexander: Committed 24 May 1851 by William Cole as a runaway. Released 24 May 1851 to P___ Eversfield.

William: Committed 26 May 1851 by James S. Buckley as a runaway. Released 10 June 1851 to John F. Chisly.

Catherine Jones: Committed 27 May 1851 by John E. Little as a runaway. Released 6 June 1851 to William W. Morrison.

Daniel: Committed 27 June 1851 by William H. Ward as a runaway. Released 12 June 1851 to C. W. Price.

Maria and child: committed 4 June 1851 by Mason Pygott for safekeeping. Released 9 June 1851 to William H, Burch.

Lydia and three children: Committed 4 June 1851 by L. H. Taylor for safekeeping. Released 5 June 1851 to William H. Brunch.

Betsy and Louisa: Committed 2 June 1851 by __ Quigley as runaways. Released 3 June 1851 To William Quigly.

Cornelius: committed 4 June 1851 by B. D. Kloffer as a runaway. Released 5 June 1851 to George W. Briscoe.

Sarah: Committed 7 June 1851 by J. W. Smith as a runaway. Released 10 June 1851 to William R. Abbott.

Orlando: Committed 7 June 1851 by James S. Buckley as a runaway. Released 123 June 1851 to Thomas D. Stone.

William Mack: Committed 7 June 1851 by Janus E. Morgan for safekeeping. Released 18 June 1851 to Michael McDermott.

Charlotte: committed 7 June 1851 by Elias Simms as runaway. Released 10 June 1851 to Elias Simms.

John Fletcher: Committed 9 June 1851by James Bowen as

runaway. Released 14 June 1851 to John S. Suit.

Robert Wood: Committed 10 June 1851 by James Bowen as a runaway. Released 21 June 1851 to William J. Bell.

George: Committed 11 June 1851 by James S. Buckley as a runaway. Released 20 June 1851 to Horace Edlin.

William: Committed 13 June 1851 by John Harris for safekeeping. Released 17 June 1851 to E. Gannon.

Oliver: Committed 19 June 1851 William M. Ward as a runaway. Released 3 July 1851 to James T. Brashers.

Mortimore: Committed 21 June 1851 by James S, Buckley as a runaway. Released 25 June 1851 to Alexander P. Hill.

Mary: Committed 20 June 1851 by E. Brooke as a runaway. Released 5 July 1851 to H. Cooke.

Carter Coats: Committed 21 June 1851 by B. D. Coffer as a runaway. Released 14 July 1851 to Bennett Green.

Austin Grier: Committed 25 June 1851 by B. D. Kloffer as a runaway. Released 30 June 1851 to J. H. B____.

Ned: Committed 4 July 1851 by James Bowen as a runaway. Released 6 July 1851 to James F. Scott.

Patrick Bell: Committed 5 July 1851 by John G. Hempler as a runaway. Released 11 July 1851 to Thomas B. Gwynn.

Matthew: Committed 8 July 1851 by Benjamin Berkley for safekeeping. Released 10 July 1851 to William H. Richards.

Henrietta: Committed 8 July 1851 by Michael Miller for safekeeping. Released 8 July 1851 to B. O. Sheckell and H. Cook.

Elizabeth: Committed 8 July 1851 by E. H. Br__ as a runaway. Released 11 July 1851 to John M. Jenkers.

John H. Dorsey: Committed 10 July 1851 by James S. Buckley as a runaway. Released 11 July 1851 to John M. Jenkers.

Milly Barnes: committed 11 July 1851 by John Cokes as a runaway. Released 23 July to Frederick Brown.

Henry Gibson: Committed 11 July 1851 as a runaway by John Adams. Released 26 July 1851 and remanded to the State of Virginia.

Thomas: Committed 12 July 1851 by James S. Buckley as a runaway. Released 24 July 1851 to J. B. Stockett.

Arch: Committed 12 July 1851 by James B. Buckley as a runaway. Released 24 July 1851 to J. B. Stockett.

Alfred: Committed 14 July 1851 by James H. Smith as a runaway. Released 22 July 1851 to J. B. Carson.

Beverly Johnson: Committed 16 July 1851 by John Smith and John S. Hale as a runaway. Released 25 July to H. D. Ashton.

George: Committed 17 July 1851 as a runaway by John Adams. Released 20 July 1851 to George W. Talbert.

Jane: committed 10 July 1851 by William Dawson for

safekeeping. Released 24 July 1851 to William G. B____.

Harriett: Committed 17 July 1851 by Robert Bowen for safekeeping. Released 21 July 1851 to B. O. Schekells and J. C. Cooke.

Ally Williams: Committed 21 July 1851 by James S. Buckley as a runaway. Released 21 July 1851 to George S. Cox.

Tom: committed 20 July 1851 by Henry Trammel for safekeeping. Released 22 July 1851 to Henry Trammel.

Tom: Committed 22 July 1851by Solomon Hubburd as a runaway. Released 23 July 1851 to Lawson Vermillion.

George Clagett: Committed 28 July 1851 by James S. Buckley as a runaway. Released 29 July 1851to Zadock Robinson.

James Marshall: Committed 29 July 1851 ty John Kelly as a runaway. Released 7 August 1851 to Charles Hill.

Richard Tyler: Committed 31 July 1851 by C. Ashland as a runaway. Released 1 August 1851 as a free man.

John H. Harris: Committed 1 August 1851 by R. R. Brown as a runaway. Released 2 August 1851 as a free man.

Vincent: Committed 5 August 1851 by James Bowen as a runaway. Released 9 August to ____.

John Henry Fields: Committed 6 August 1851 by James Lynch as a runaway. Released 30 August to George Hunter Jr.

Robert Johnson: Committed 9 August 1851 by Jane C. H.

Scott for safekeeping. Released 30 August 1851 to ____ & Hill.

Arthur Alexander: Committed 10 August 1851 by A. E. L. Kerse as a runaway. Released 1 September 1851to Allan Taylor.

Nace: Committed 12 August 1851 by Joshua Lloyd as a runaway. Released 1 September 1851 to Justin Richardson.

Charlotte: Committed 12 August 1851 by John A. ___ for safekeeping Released 13 August 1851 to R. J. Bowen.

Rachael: Committed 13 August 1851 by B. Mackell for safekeeping. Released 1 September 1851 to S. T. Stonestreet.

Wallace: Committed 14 August 1851 by James Kyser as a runaway. Released 16 August 1851 to John H. Mackey.

Martha: Committed 18 August 1851 by M. w. Ward as a runaway. Released 19 August 1851 to E. Bowen.

Frances Daley: Committed 18 August 1851 by B. D. Klopfer as a runaway. Released 30 August 1851 to O. C. Wight.

Emeline: Committed 19 August 1851 by B. D. Klopfer as a runaway. Released 27 August 1851 to J. W. Lathan/Latham.

Jonas Gallaway: Committed 20 August 1851 by A. E. L. Kess/Keese as a runaway. Released 26 August 1851 to O. B. Suit.

Joseph Pinney: Committed 22 August 1851 by A. E. L. Keese/Kess for safekeeping. Released 2 September 1851 to James Throckmorton.

Luke: Committed 25 August 1851 for safekeeping Released 26 August 1851.

Chloe Ann Stevenson: Committed 3 September 1851 by John Davis as a runaway. Released 6 September 1851 to William A. Wallace and Brian Hill.

John: Committed 5 September 1851 by B. D. Klopfer as a runaway. Released 10 September 1851 to R. W. W. Bowie.

Henry Jackson: Committed 8 September 1851 by J. H. Craig as a runaway. Released 19 September 1851 to Horatio Fennell.

William: Committed 18 September 1851 by B. Klopfer as a runaway. Released 9 September 1851 to William Wilson.

Thomas Wilson: Committed 11 September 1851 by J. B. Frazier as a runaway. Released 15 September 1851 to Thomas H. Kent.

James Bond: Committed 11 September 1851 by J. B. Frazier as a runaway. Released 15 September 1851 to Thomas H. Kent.

Amy: Committed 19 September 1851 by R. T. Mills as a runaway. Released to William A. Smith.

Hilliary Lemon: Committed 22 September 1851 by J. W. Wright as a runaway. Released 23 September to George W. Lowry/Lorry.

Henry: Committed 23 September 1851 by James Rustridge as a runaway. Released 25 September 1851 to Samuel T. Berry.

Maria Marshall & child: Committed 1 October 1851 by T. Wheeler for safekeeping. Released 22 October 1851.

Alowises: Committed 2 October 1851 by Phil. Oterbach Jr. as a runaway. Released 28 1851 to John R. Fergerson.

George: Committed 6 October 1851 as a runaway by A. H. Craig. Released 18 October 1851 to H. G. Wilson.

Sopiah: Committed 13 October 1851 by B. D. Klopfer as a runaway. Released 18 October to A. H. Mill.

Ellen: committed 16 October 1851 by William H. Bainalls & R. R. Burr. As a runaway. Released 23 October 1851 to R. D. Beall.

Gabriel: Committed 21 October 1851 by B. D. Klopfer as a runaway. Released 30 October 1851.

David Castes: Committed 22 October 1851 by Joshua ___ as a runaway. Released 28 November as free.

E. Brown: Committed 23 October 1851 as a runaway by P. B. Bell. Released 27 October 1851 to M. Wright.

Samuel Jackson: Committed 30 October 1851 by H. T. L. Wilson as a runaway. Released 3 November 1851 to Owen Capel.

Fanny Harvey: Committed 31 October 1851 by M. Powell for safekeeping. Released 11 November 1851 to Markland.

Jacob Gantt: committed 7 November 1851 BY B. D. Klopfer as a runaway. Released 11 November 1851 to John Newton.

Sarah Ann: Committed 10 November 1851 by William H. Barnach as a runaway. Released 11 December 1851 to Selby Spriggs/Spaggs.

Robert alis George alias James: Committed 11 November 1851 by William H. Barnach as a runaway. Released 15 November 1851 to H. A. White & A. Fleming.

Charles Johnson: Committed 11 November 1851 by B. D. Klopfer as a runaway Released 17 November to F. Marklin.

Nace Brown: Committed 15 November 1851 by James Bean as a runaway. Released 17 November 1851 to John Surrett.

Charles Mason: committed 19 November 1851 by William H. Barnach as a runaway. Released 19 November 1851 to J. D. Reade.

Sarah Jackson; Committed 22 November 1851 by E. Sampson for safekeeping. Release not noted.

Sophy: Committed 26 November 1851 by James Bowan as a runaway. Released 10 December 1851 to E, H. _____ and George F. Richards.

Jemina Johnson: Committed 26 November 1851 by James H. Smith as a runaway. Released 23 January 1852 to John W. Donn.

Hannah: Committed 27 November 1851 by John Davis for safekeeping. Released 29 November to William Steel.

Rachael Shields: Committed 1 December 1851 by F. A. Jones & J. W. Hatcher as a runaway. Released February 5 1852 to E. E. Stonestreet.

Nelly: Committed 22 December 1851 by John Adams for safekeeping. Released 23 December 1851 to "self".

Edward Loung: Committed 22 December 1851 by Timothy O'Neal for safekeeping. Released 27 December 1851 to Timothy O'Neal.

Cornelius: Committed 23 December 1851 by R, H, Sedgewick for safekeeping. Released 1 January 1852 to R. H. Sedgewick.

Enoch: Committed 25 December 1851 by James Bowine/as a runaway. Released 10 January 1852 to D. R. Byer.

Lloyd: Committed 2 January 1852 by James S. Buckley as a runaway. Released 9 January 1852 to G. T. Murrow.

Lewis: Committed 5 January 1852 for safekeeping by Robert Bowie. Released 23 January 1852 to Edward Horne.

Ann Marie: Committed as a runaway by W. W. Ward 5 January 1852. Released to John Bettinger 12 January 1852.

Lewis: Committed as a runaway by J. W. Wright 5 January 1852. Released E. N. Roach/Rush January 1852.

Richard F. Gantt: Committed as a runaway by Joseph B. Gray 10 January 1852. Released B. O. Spaulding 15 January 1852.

Robert: Committed as a runaway by W. W. Ward 5 January 1852. Released to E. B. Ball 13 January 1852.

Frank: Committed as a runaway by B. D. Klopfer 15 January

1852. Released to H. C. Matthews 12 January 1852.

Nace: Committed as a runaway by James H. Smith 5 January 1852. Released to B. O. Sheckells 20 January 1852.

Lewis Barnes: Committed as a runaway by James Ross 21 January 1852. Released 21 January 1852. (Explanation of release is illegible)

James Henderson: Committed as a runaway by J. F. Wollard 21 January 1852. Released to John W. Mullikin 17 February 1852.

George W. Dyson: Committed as a runaway by William Lewis 7 February 1852. Released to John E. Neale 17 February 1852.

Charlotte: Committed as a runaway by James H. Smith 8 February 1852. Released to James C. Dyer 10 February 1852.

Elias: Committed as a runaway by W. W. Ward 9 February 1852. Released to Elbert Shaw 13 February 1852.

Eliza: Committed as a runaway by Worthington 9 February 1852. Released to Worthington 12 February 1852.

Richard Smallwood: Committed as a runaway by James Bowan 10February 1852. Released to J. R. Jackson 16 February 1852.

Isabella Graham: Committed as a runaway by Isaac Stoddus 12 February 1852. Released as free 27 February 1852.

Dick: Committed as a runaway by Francis Lacy 16 February 1852. Released to Walter A. Wilkinson 18 February 1852.

Richard Chase: Committed as a runaway by himself 1 8 February 1852. Released to himself 18 February 1852.

Tom: Committed for safekeeping by Beverly Forck_19 February 1852. Released 21 February 1852.

Thomas Price: Committed for safekeeping by Thomas Athey 19 February 1852. Released 3 March 1852 by order of Thomas Hunter.

Milly: Committed as a runaway by B. Klopfer 21 February 1852. Released to George Thompson 22 February 1852.

Rachail: Committed as a runaway by W. M. Ward 21 February 1852. Released to Jackson Morton 27 February 1852.

Hamilton Sampson: Committed for safekeeping 14 February 1852 by C. Miller. Released 21 February to M. Rooison.

Matilda: Committed for safekeeping 27 February 1852 by William A. Watton. Released 17 March 1852 to James T. Perkins.

Celia: Committed for safekeeping by R. R. Burr 1 March 1852. Released 4 March 1852 to W. H. Ward.

Delila: Committed 1 March 1852 by Edward M. Duvall. Released 1 March 1852 to E. M. Duvall.

William: Committed 1 March 1852 as a runaway by William Cooke. Released 8 March 1852 to Francis Norris.

Sandy Loring: Committed 23 March 1852 by S. B. Scaggs . Released 15 April to S. B. Scaggs.

Sarah: Committed 3 April 1852 by James Bowie as a runaway. Released 8 April 1852 to Richard F. Hall.

Fanny & child: Committed 8 April 1852 by B. D. Klopfer as a runaway. Released 9 April 1852 to N. C. Dickerson.

John: Committed by B. D. Klopfer as a runaway. Released 1 May 1852 to J. M. Toming.

Charles Haley: by B. D. Klopfer as a runaway. Released 20 April 1852 as a free man.

Thomas Williams: Committed by John Robey 23 April 1852 as a runaway. Released 26 April 1852 to Samuel W. Williams.

Michael: Committed by B. D. Klopfer as a runaway 24 April 1852. Released 26 April 1852 to Charles Hill.

Ike: Committed 28 April 1852 by John A. Smith for safekeeping. Released 8 May 1852.

Harriet Carter: Committed by J. W. Busher as a runaway. Released 3 May 1852 to Phillip Stone.

Sidney Smith: Committed by Mary M. Sheridan 3 May 1852 for safekeeping. Released 5 May 1852 to George Richards.

Ignatious: Committed 6 May 1852 by C. Buckhead as a runaway. Released 10 May 1852 to E. H. Jackson.

Thomas Wheeler: Committed 8 May 1852 by John Conally as a runaway. Released 15 May 1852 to D. R. Dyer.

Fanny Hawkins: Committed 11 May 1852 by James Donnogher for safekeeping. Released 19 May 1852.

Alexander Johnson: Committed 11 May 1852 for safekeeping by William Dawson. Released 12 May 1852 to William Dawson for Elizabeth Williams.

Louisa: Committed 12 May 1852 by William H. Bernardo for safekeeping. Released 17 May 1852 to William H. Bernardo.

Horace: Committed 14 May 1852 by J. M. Busher for safekeeping. Released 15 May 1852.

Louis: Committed 14 May 1852 as a runaway by William W. Ward. Released 19 May 1852 to William R. Ross.

Emely & Aley: Committed 14 May 1852 by Sarah King for safekeeping. Released 17 May 1852.

Caleb Snowden: Committed 18 May 1852 as a runaway by Isaac Scroggin. Released 20 May 1852 as a free man.

Paul Brown: Committed 22 May 1852 by J. W. Wright for safekeeping. Released 24 May 1852 to J. W. Wright.

Joe Hall: Committed 22 May 1852 by E. B. Duvall as a runaway. Released 24 May 1852 to Henry D. Ellen.

Nancy Howard: Committed 27 May 1852 for safekeeping by M. Sauter. Released 3 June 1852 to John C. Cook.

John Jackson: Committed 28 May 1852 by Jacob E. Gross as a runaway. Released 28 May 1852 to J. H. Calowell.

Priscilla & Mary Ann Sewell: Committed 2 June 1852 by Dennis Calahan for safe-keeping. Released 3 June 1852 to E. C. Rowles.

Robert: Committed by Charles
Turnbull 2 June 1852 as a
runaway. Released 4 June 1852
to William Lyles.

Washington: Committed by
Charles Turnbull 2 June 1852
as a runaway. Released 4 June
1852 to William Lyles.

John: Committed by I. H. Smith 2
June 1852 as a runaway.
Released 5 June 1852 to A. L.
Berry.

Nace Brown: Committed by
William H. Ward 2 June 1852
as a runaway. Released 5 June
1852 to Benjamin Taylor.

Mary: Committed by 6 June 1852
as a runaway. Released 10 June
1852 to Frank Hall.

Julia: Committed 6 June 1852 by
William ____ as a runaway.
Released 9 January 1852 to
Frank Hall.

Nace: Committed 9 June 1852 as a
runaway by James Owen.
Released 17 June 1852 to
William Branshaw.

Rufus Jackson: Committed 1852
by John Adams as a runaway.
Released 11 June 1852 to
Thomas M. Offit.

Thomas John: Committed 10 June
1852 by William Houston as a
runaway. Released 12 June
1852 to S. Blandford.

Henry Bowie: Committed 12 June
1852 by M. Martin as a
runaway. Released 21June 1852
to Simon Welch.

Nelly: Committed for safekeeping
by N. Callan 3 July 1852.
Released to J. B. H. Fulton 9
July 1852.

Robert: Committed 6 July 1852 by
John E. DeWitt as a runaway.

Released 9 July 1852 to James
C. Dyer.

Charles Herbert: Committed
7 July 1852 by as a runaway by
Robert T. Mills. Released 12
July 1852 to Charles Hill.

Charles: Committed 29 June 1852
by W. M. Ward as a runaway.
Released 1 July 1852 to R. F.
Hall.

Frank: Committed 30 June 1852
by E. E. Buckley as a runaway.
Released 2 July 1852 to James
Lewelyn.

Nick: Committed 23 July 1852 by
James S. Buckley as a runaway.
Released 2 August 1852 to A.
W. Boone.

John: Committed 25 July 1852 by
R. Mills as a runaway. Released
27 July 1852 to A. N. Walls.

Thomas: Committed 26 July 1852
for safekeeping by George W.
Young Released to William
Robey 26 July 1852.

Mahala: Committed 26 July1852
by Henry A. Klopfer as a
runaway. Released 29 July
1852 to George T. Richards.

William Scott: Committed 29 July
1852 by John L. Fowler as a
runaway. Released
7 September 1852 as free.

Rezin: Committed 27 July 1852 for
safekeeping by K. Suit. .
Released 7 August 1852 to J. J.
Forbes.

John T. Hamilton: Committed
31 July 1852 by C. D. Martin
for safekeeping. Released 1
August 1852 to C. D. Martin.

Alfred: Committed 2 August 1852
by J. A. Willelt as a runaway.
Released 5 August 1852 to
Charles T. Porter.

Tom: Committed 5 August 1852
by E. Burnett for safekeeping.
Released 9 August 1852 to
Edward Horne.

Edith: Committed 6 August 1852
by William W. Ward as a
runaway. Released 12 August
1852 to Isaac Estell.

Ned Wimms (Williams?):
Committed 6 August 1852 by
J. W. Atchinson as a runaway.
Released 1852 to L. Mitchell.

Sconey: Committed 7 August 1852
for safekeeping by
Jackson Morton. Released 9
Septemebr 1852 to
Jackson Morton.

Mary & child: Committed
10 August 1852 for safekeeping
by Ed. Horn. Released 10
August 1852 to S. I. Little.

Richard: Committed 11 August
1852 for safekeeping by C. D.
Martin. Released 18 August
1852 to E. Horne.

Jacob: Committed 14 August 1852
for safekeeping by John Davis.
Released 13 August 1852.

Thomas Henny: Committed
18 August 1852 by J. S.
Buckley as a runaway. Released
1852 to John A. Brooks.

Robert Diggs: Committed
18 August 1852 by J. S.
Buckley as a runaway. Released
1852 to John A. Brooks.

Hamlett: Committed 20 August
1852 by Charles Kemmell as a
runaway. Released 23 August
1852 to William Hughes.

Harrison: Committed 22 August
1852 by ___ Blake as a
runaway.Released 24 August
1852 to Duff Green Jr.

Matthew: Committed 23 August
1852 for safekeeping by

Edward Horne. Released
1 September 1852 to Edward
Horne.

David Baker: Committed
24 August 1852 for safekeeping
by F. B. Plummer. Released 2
September to F. B. Plummer.

Matilda: Committed 30 August
1852 by Adam Davison as a
runaway. Released 1 September
1852 to James Branaugh.

Susan Sayers: Committed
31 August 1852 by
Isaac Stoddard as a runaway.
Released 7 September 1852 as
free.

Jess: Committed 2 September 1852
for safekeeping by E. Horne.
Released 23 September 1852 to
E. Horne.

Martha: Committed 3 September
1852 for safekeeping by
William Clarke. Released 5
September 1852 to William
Clarke.

Robert: Committed 10 September
1852 for safekeeping by E.
Horne. Released 23 September
1852 to E. Horne.

Henny Finney: Committed
13 September 1852 by Allen
Selby as a runaway. Released to
Thomas E. France
13 September 1852.

Ally, Ned, Stany, Nat , Patrick:
Committed 11 September 1852
by J. S. Buckley as a runaways.
Released 29 September 1852 to
Joseph H. Bradley Jr.

Joe Beale: Committed
12 September 1852 by John
Adams as a runaway. Released
29 September 1852 to Joseph
H. Bradley Jr.

Robert: Committed 13 September
1852 by B. D. Klopfer.

Released 29 September 1852 to
Joseph H. Bradley Jr.

Jeffrey: Committed 13 September
1852 by B. D. Klopfer.
Released 29 September 1852 to
Joseph H. Bradley Jr.

Tom: Committed 13 September
1852 by James S. Buckley.
Released 14 September 1852 to
Lewis Mackall.

Louisa: Committed 14 September
1852 for safekeeping by R. B.
Lee. Released 1 October 1852
to _ E. Robey.

Horace: Committed 16 September
1852 for safekeeping by
Gustavas Waters. Released 20
September 1852 to Gustavas
Waters.

Horace: Committed 16 September
1852 by James Bowen as a
runaway. Released 7 October
1852 to G. White.

Tom: Committed 16 September
1852 as a runaway by Emanuel
Lacy. Released 20 September
1852 to William Martin.

Rebecca and 3 children:
Committed 21 September 1852
for safekeeping by William
Carlisle. Discharged 9 May
1853.

Sandy: Committed 21 September
1852 as a runaway by Francis
Goddard. Released 22
September to E. R. Byrne.

Hilliary: Committed 22 September
1852 as a runaway by James S.
Buckley. Released 24
September 1852 to George W.
Loring/Long.

Hilliary: Committed 25 September
1852 as a runaway by James S.
Buckley. Released 28
September 1852 to ____
Mosher.

Charles Jackson: Committed
28 September 1852 for
safekeeping by Alan H. Smith.
Released 2 October to
Alan H. Smith.

Lewis Washington Alexandria:
Committed 30 September 1852
as a runaway by William
Magee. Released 1 October
1852 to J. W. Barker.

Mary Minor: Committed
2 October 1852 as a runaway by
Reese & Cox. Released 11
October 1852 to F. Warner.

William: Committed 2 October
1852 as a runaway by W. W.
Ward. Released 13 October
1852 to William D. Bowie and
J. E. Jones.

Charles Henry: Committed
8 October 1852 as a runaway by
William Lloyd. Released 18
October to J. F. Summers.

Ned: Committed 11 October 1852
as a runaway by J. H. Smith.
Released 12 October 1852 to J.
Z. Jenkins.

Harriet Jones: Committed
13 October 1852 as a runaway
by J. W. Bucher. Released 16
October 1852 to William H.
Purdie.

Charles: Committed 13 October
1852 as a runaway by J. H.
Smith. Released 19 October
1852 to P. W. Athey.

Henry Simms: Committed
18 October 1852 for
safekeeping by William P.
Cannon. Released 19 October
1852 to Cassandra Evans.

Susan and male child: Committed
28 October 1852 for
safekeeping by Robert Bowie.
Released 31 October 1852 to
John E. Robey.

Henry Stewart: Committed 28 October 1852 as a runaway by David Waters. Released 4 November 1852 to M. B. Cooke.

Harriet & Child: Committed 29 October 1852 as a runaway by James S. Buckley. Released 1 November 1852 to Edwin Watson.

Isaac: Committed 1 November 1852 as a runaway by James Bowers. Released 18 November 1852 to Robert Claggett.

John: Committed 2 November 1852 as a runaway by M. M. Ward. Released 16 November 1852 to George A. Mitchell.

Robert & John Johnson: Committed 4 November 1852 for safekeeping by F. A. Jones. Released 15 November 1852 to F. A. Jones.

Bill: Committed 6 November 1852 for safekeeping by H. R. Merryman. Released 6 November 1852 to H. R. Merryman.

Ned: Committed 15 November 1852 for safekeeping by William Clark. Released 20 November 1852 to J. S. Buckley.

Joe Simms: Committed 13 November 1852 as a runaway by J. W. Smith. Released 15 November 1852 to George W. Tomey.

Peter: Committed 29 November 1852 as a runaway by M. M. Ward. Released 15 December 1852 to Samuel West.

Eliza Watkins: Committed 29 November 1852 as a runaway by Michael Quigley. Released 2 December 1852 to George A. Diggs.

Jesse Nelson: Committed 30 November 1852 for safekeeping by John Carmichael. Released January 15, 1852 to John F. Ennis, his attorney.

Fudge: Committed 30 November 1852 for safekeeping by U. S. Marshall. Released 14 December by U. S. Marshall.

Anthony: Committed 3 December 1852 as a runaway by James S. Buckley. Released 4 December 1852 to J. F. Perry.

Henry Lynch: Committed 7 December as a runaway by William H. Libby. Released 11 December 1852 to Lawrence Allnutt.

Rezin: Committed 9 December 1852 for safekeeping by Rachel B. Bernard. Released 10 December to James E. Robey.

Lelia: Committed 9 December 1852 for safekeeping by E. H. Edlin. Released 13 December 1852 to E. H. Edlin.

Rachael: Committed 11 December 1852 for safekeeping by U. S. Marshall. Released 14 December by U. S. Marshall.

Mary Boon/Boone: Committed 27 December 1852 for safekeeping by Owen Conley. Released 1 January 1853 to Owen Connally.

Bob: Committed 30 December 1852 as a runaway by John Freer. Released 6 January 1853 to Z. B. Beall

Adam: Committed 31 December 1852 as a runaway by James Bardine. Released 3 January 1853 to Thomas H. Osburn.

George: Committed 31 December 1852 as a runaway by James Bardine. Released 3 January 1853 to Thomas H. Osburn.

Hanson: Committed 31 December 1852 as a runaway by James Bardine. Released 3 January 1853 to Thomas H. Osburn.

John: Committed 31 December 1852 as a runaway by Milton M. Ward. Released 6 January 1853 to John L. Belt.

Sam: Committed 2 January 1853 as a runaway by Benjamin Thorn. Released 5 January 1853 to John Loung.

Jim: Committed 2 January 1853 as a runaway by Benjamin Thorn. Released 5 January 1853 to John Loung.

Daniel Hayney: Committed 9 December 1852 for safekeeping by J. W. Manikin. Released 8 January 1853 to George M. Hunter.

Harriet: Committed 5 January 1853 for safekeeping by Z. B. Beall. Released 6 January 1853 to Z, B. Beall.

Emeline: Committed 9 January 1853 as a runaway by William Barnes. Released 11 January 1853 to George A. Mitchell.

Sandy: Committed 11 January 1853 as a runaway by Thomas Piles. Released 21 January 1853 to Thomas S. Edelin.

Samuel Lumby: Committed 11 January 1853 as a runaway by A. E. L. Reese. Released 4 March 1853 to G. H. Waters.

Stephen: Committed 22 January 1853 as a runaway by J. F. Wollard. Released 23 January 1853 to William Berry of Benjamin.

Singleton: Committed 23 January 1853 as a runaway by Robert P. Mills. Released 26 January 1853 to_____ Crop.

Stephen Ambush: Committed 22 January 1853 as a runaway by John H. Neal. Released 23 January 1853 to

Maria Young: Committed 24 January 1853 as Committed 5 January 1853 for safekeeping by by A. E. L. Reese. Released 22 January 1853 to E. E. Morgan for Robinson.

Thomas Day: Committed 5 January 1853 for safekeeping by Henry Trunnell. Released 27 January 1853 to Rezin Stephens.

Thomas Handon: Committed 28 January 1853 for safekeeping by R. K. Lambell. Released to R. K. Lambell.

Ned: Committed 2 February 1853 as a runaway by R. T. Mills. Released 8 February to J. F. Fait.

Sarah Elizabeth: Committed 6 February 1853 as a runaway by James Bowen. Released 8 February to J. F. Fait.

Jane: Committed 4 February 1853 for safekeeping by Herndon Fowler. Released 7 March to James Nokes Jr.

Thomas: Committed 4 February 1853 for safekeeping by Gustavas Waters. Released 12 February to Gustavas Waters.

Francis Williams: Committed 14 February 1853 as a runaway by William A. Bass and William H. Barnoels. Released as free.

Michael Reed: Committed 18 February 1853 for safekeeping by John C. Bunche. Released 9 March 1853 to John C. Bunche.

Ellick: Committed 22 February 1853 as a runaway by James Bowen. Released 24 February to James C. Isaac.

Benjamin Wilson: Committed 24 February 1853 as a runaway by William Corse. Released 14 March 1853 as a free man.

Mary Ellen: Committed 24 February 1853 as a runaway by John Adams. Released 2 March 1853 to Thomas M. Offet.

Richard: Committed 25 February 1853 for safekeeping by John Adams. Released 25 February 1853.

Maria & child: Committed 25 February 1853 for safekeeping by F. G. Skirvan. Released 2 March to "self".

Louisa & child: Committed 2 March 1853 as a runaway by Charles Kinnard. Released 3 March 1853 to P. W. Evensfield.

John: Committed 7 March 1853 as a runaway by James Ennis. Released 17 March 1853 to William A. _____.

Mary: Committed 8 March 1853 as a runaway by Reson Stevens. Released 6 April 1853 to Thomas L. Offett.

Hamilton: Committed 14 March 1853 for safekeeping by James Bowen. Released 18 March 1853 to J. E. Robey.

Hilliary Lemmons: Committed 18 January 1853 as a runaway by Thomas King. Released 22 January 1853 to Theodore Mosher.

Charlotte & child: Committed 17 March 1853 for safekeeping by W. G. White. Released 21 March to J. E. Florence.

John: Committed 20 March 1853 as a runaway by Thomas H. Ratcliff. Released 21 March to Greenberg M. Watson.

Robert: Committed 22 March 1853 for safekeeping by William Cox. Released 29 March 1853 to C. S. Wallack.

Rachael: Committed 23 March 1853 for safekeeping by John France. Released to John Strunser.

John Taylor: Committed 28 March 1853 as a runaway by James Ennis. Released 28 March 1853 to C. S. Richards.

Eleanor Barton: Committed 29 March 1853 as a runaway by William Cox. Released 1 April as free.

Eliza: Committed 20 March 1853 as a runaway by W. W. Ward. Released 1 April 1853 to J. E. Robey.

Michael: Committed 20 March 1853 as a runaway by W. W. Ward. Released 1 April 1853 to B. O. & R. G. Sheckells.

Billy Williams alias John Isaacs: Committed 31 March 1853 for safekeeping by William Cox. Released 4 April 1853 to Moses P. Donaldson.

Kitty: Committed 3 April 1853 as a runaway by R. T. Mills. Released 4 April 1853 to E. Magruder.

James & Henry: Committed 7 April 1853 as a runaway by James S. Buckley. Released

9 April 1853 to Richard F. Tubman.

John: Committed 7 April 1853 as a runaway by R. T. Mills. Released 10 April !853 to William G. Lamar.

Sam Hawkins: Committed 7 April 1853 as a runaway by A. E. L. Kuse. Released 10 April 1853 not confirmed as a runaway.

Moses: Committed 9 April 1853 as a runaway by George W,.Briscoe. Released 9 April 1853 to George W. Briscoe.

Emily Baker: Committed 10 April 1853 for safekeeping by Hamilton J. Smith. Released 19 Smith to John C. Smith.

Martha: Committed 10 April 1853 as a runaway by H. W. Porter. Released 12 April 1853 to H. W. Porter.

Basil: Committed 14 April 1853 as a runaway by Thomas J. Beall. Released 19 April 1853 to Thomas J. Beall.

Jane Douglass: Committed 15 April 1853 as a runaway by W. M. Ward. Released 15 April to Lewis Mackill.

William Nelson: Committed 19 April 1853 for safekeeping by Mrs. Earl Cooleridge. Released 25 April 1853 to A. Keech Jr.

Harry Hill: Committed 22 April 1853 as a runaway by W. W. Ward. Released 28 April 1853 to J. B. Beall.

Rosetta Davis: Committed 24 April 1853 as a runaway by Henry Wood. Released 28 1853 to James Roberson.

Henry Johnson: Committed 28 April 1853 for safekeeping by Smith Thompson. Released

30 April 1853 to John H. Carlson.

Francis: Committed 28 April 1853 for safekeeping by Henry Tucker. Released 29 April 1853 to Calvert Brown.

Sarah Plummer: Committed 28 April 1853 as a runaway by A. E. L. Reise. Released 25 May 1853 as a free woman.

Ameline: Committed 29 April 1853 as a runaway by W. W. Ward. Released 17 May 1853 to George Kephaus.

Basil: Committed 5 May 1853 for safekeeping by John F. Boon. Released 17 May 1853 to H. H. Lewis.

Ann: Committed 11 May 1853 for safekeeping by F. S. Key. Released 10 May 1853 to F. S. Key. [2]

George: Committed 11 May 1853 as a runaway by James Bowen. Released 23 May 1853 to A. B. Berry.

Elbert: Committed 13 May 1853 as a runaway by James Bowen. Released 14 May 1853 to John Adams.

Phillip: Committed 15 May 1853 for safekeeping by W. J. Brooke. Released 23 May 1853 to R. C. Brooke.

James: Committed 16 May 1853 as a runaway by John Frier. Released 16 May 1853 as a "Bound Boy".

Mary: Committed 18 May 1853 as a runaway by R. T. Mills. Released 19 May 1853 to R. N. Darnell.

Matilda: Committed 30 May 1853 as a runaway by James A.

---

[2] Francis Scott Key ????

31

Matte. Released 1 June 1853 to Robert Crunch.

Charles Brown: Committed 4 June 1853 as a runaway by John Davis. Released 13 June 1853 to Fred Bates.

Chester E. A. Chase: Committed 6 June 1853 as a runaway by E. A. Jones. Released 22 June 1853 after proving his freedom.

Simon: Committed 20 June 1853 for safekeeping by William Kimball. Released 5 September 1853 to William Corse.

Cornelia: Committed 24 June 1853 for safekeeping by Isaac h. Ward. Released 12 July 1853 to R. A. B. Mann.

Robert: Committed 1 July 1853 as a runaway by James W. Buckley. Released 14 July 1853 to Robert W. Brook.

Albert: Committed 1 July 1853 as a runaway by J. F. Wollard. Released 14 July 1853 to E. Gorden.

William: Committed 7 July 1853 as a runaway by James Talbot. Released 9 July 1853 to J. C. Trent.

Mary Batson & child: Committed 12 July 1853 as a runaway by Kessy Atchison. Released 27 July 1853 to R. E. Jankins.

Charles Brown: Committed 9 July 1853 for safekeeping by Fred Bates. Released 4 August 1853 to John Davis.

John Claggett: Committed 10 July 1853 for safekeeping by John T. Buckley. Released 16 July 1853 to John T. Buckley.

James Bowman: Committed 16 July 1853 as a runaway William Mulloy. Released 19 July 1853 to G. W. Young.

Ann Maria Gray alias Butler: Committed 18 July 1853 as a runaway by A. E. L. Reese. Released 24 July to William B. Compton.

Richard Low: Committed 19 July 1853 as a runaway by Bailey Brown. Released 21 July 1853 to J. B. Belt.

Ned Webster: Committed 20 July 1853 as a runaway by F. W. Colelazier. Released 27 July 1853 to J. A. Washington.

Ned & Charles Hawkins: Committed 20 July 1853 as runaways by William Pasquett. Released 21 July 1853 to E. Eversfield.

Charles H. Selby: Committed 20 July 1853 as a runaway by William Pasquett. Released 25 July 1853 to John F. Summers.

Nelly: Committed 21 July 1853 as a runaway by John A. Millet. Released 22 July 1853 to John Townsend.

Emeline: Committed 21 July 1853 as a runaway by John A. Millet. Released as free 21 July 1853.

William Duckett: Committed 21 July 1853 as a runaway by John A. Millet. Released 23 July to I. G. Alder .

Bill: Committed 21 July 1853 as a runaway by A. Lattoritte. Released 23 July 1853 to Elizabeth Wilson.

Kitty: Committed 24 July 1853 as a runaway by R. Y. Mills. Released 27 July 1853 to C. R. Belt.

Micenta: Committed 24 July 1853 as a runaway by R. Y. Mills. Released 27 July 1853 to C. R. Belt.

Jeff: Committed 26 July 1853 as a runaway by James M. Buckley. Released 28 July 1853 to J. D. Deitley.

Osbourne: Committed 6 August 1853 as a runaway by James W. Allen. Released 16 August 1853 to J. C. McG___.

Caroline: Committed 10 August 1853 for safekeeping by E. C. Dyer. Released 13 August 1853 to Mrs. W. H. Williams.

Eliza Lee: Committed 6 August 1853 as a runaway by J. H. Wise. Released 15 August 1853 to L. Lamhorn.

Edward Rumsey: Committed 15 August 1853 as a runaway by Isaac Stoddard. Released 22 August 1853 as free.

Amanda: Committed 20 August 1853 for safekeeping by William Jones. Released 27 August 1853 to Joseph B___.

Charles Berry: Committed 22 August 1853 as a runaway by P. B. Beall Released 30 August 1853 as free.

Sam: Committed 27 August 1853 as a runaway by Charles ___. Released 31 August 1853 to William W. Hill.

Sarah: Committed 30 August 1853 for safekeeping by Edgar H. Bates. Released 5 September 1853 to William Case.

Mandy: Committed 2 September 1853 for safekeeping by Alexander H. Young. Released 14 September 1853 to B. A. Sheckall.

Salley: Committed 3 September 1853 for safekeeping by D. W. Kent. Released 5 September 1853 to Joseph Brown.

Jack Jews: Committed 3 September 1853 as a runaway by James H. Simon. Released 5 September 1853 to George W. S___.

Betsy: Committed 4 September 1853 as a runaway by R. R. B___. Released 8 September 1853 to A. Bowie.

Maria: Committed 14 September 1853 for safekeeping by J. W. Blount. Released 28 May 1854 to Hon. J. Morton.

Mary Ann Lacy: Committed 16 September 1853 as a runaway by C. Kimmell. Released 20 September 1853 to J. J. Fobes.

Sarah Panay: Committed 14 September 1853 for safekeeping by Francis R. Darnell. Released 23 September 1853 to John C. Cook.

Eliza Tolson: Committed 19 September 1853 as a runaway by B. W. Bell. Released 19 September 1853 upon being proven free.

Andrew _____: Committed 22 September 1853 as a runaway by William Fletcher. Released 22 September 1853 to P. H. Minor.

Amos Washington: Committed 24 September 1853 as a runaway by Davis Barnells. Released 30 September to B. W. Brawner.

Ferde: Committed 25 September 1853 for safekeeping by J. E. Morgan. Released 28 September to B. O. Sheckle.

E___ W. Koy: Committed 27 September 1853 as a runaway by Edward Krouse.

Released 13 October 1853 to William H. Harrison.

Isaac: Committed 4 October 1853 as a runaway. Released 25 October 1853 to Robert Claggett.

Susan Kent: Committed 13 October 1853 as a runaway by F. W. Coldlazier. Released 2 December 1853 to Richard Beckett.

_____ **Dorsey:** Committed 15 October 1853 for safekeeping by Thomas C. Magruder. Released 26 May 1854 to J. C. Cook.

Maria: Committed 19 October 1853 as a runaway by John P. Keif. Released 25 October 1853 to Benjamin Darnell.

Edward Watson: Committed 20 October 1853 as a runaway by Robert Waters. Released 17 November 1853 to Alfred Bell.

Ellen: Committed 20 October 1853 as a runaway by B. W. Beall. Released 22 October 1853 to J. A. Washington.

Thomas Wills: Committed 22 October 1853 as a runaway by George Krouse. Released 25 October 1835 having proven his freedom.

Eliza Ann: Committed 26 October 1853 as a runaway by James H. Buck. Released 7 November 1853 to Robert Claggett.

Caroline: Committed 2 November 1853 as a runaway by James Simpson. Released 16 November 1853 to Margaret E. E. Oliver.

Robert Henry Young: Committed 2 November 1853 as a runaway by William A. Bass. Released 16 November 1853 to John K. Garrison.

Peyton Mahoney: Committed 4 November 1853 as a runaway by William H. Barnach. Released 5 November 1853 as a free man.

Henry Green: Committed 4 November 1853 as a runaway by William H. Barnach. Released 11 December 1853 to _____ Keill.

Henry Stewart: Committed 14 November 1853 as a runaway by George Hutton. Died in jail 23 November 1853.

Samuel Stephens: Committed 15 November 1853 as a runaway by Isaac Buck. Released 16 November to Brooke B. Williams.

Frank Arnold: Committed 19 November 1853 as a runaway. Released 17 February 1853 to H. P. Howard.

James Flint : Committed 22 November 1853 as a runaway by William Lloyde. Released 12 December 1853 to B. O. Taylor.

Richard: Committed 23 November 1853 as a runaway. Released 24 November 1853 to James C. Sommers.

Rubin Dorsey: Committed 23 November 1853 as a runaway by I. S. Willett. Released 30 November 1853 as a free man.

Arthur: Committed 24 November 1853 for safekeeping by F. Magruder. Released 25 November 1853 to James Brown.

Bob Johnson: Committed 30 November 1853 for safekeeping. Released 27 December 1853 to M. Aoles.

Milly, ___, and John: Committed 1 December 1853 as runaways by A. Gatmiller. Released 7 December 1853 to John Hoover.

Robert Johnson: Committed 29 November 1853 for safekeeping by Morris Adler. Entry noted as a "mistake".[3]

Ned Lee: Committed 5 December 1853 as a runaway by H. L. L. Wilson. Released 14 December 1853 to Washington ____

Clem Wilson: Committed 13 December 1853 as a runaway by G. W. Walkins. Released 19 December 1853 to R. S. Dunlap and John Adams.

Charles Johnson: Committed 15 December 1853 for safekeeping by Sophia Barry. Released 23 December 1853 to Sophia Barry.

Henry: Committed 17 December 1853 for safekeeping by William Duvall. Released 19 December 1853 to William Duvall.

Dennis Harrison: Committed 13 December 1853 as a runaway by Isaac Birch. Released 3 January 1854 to A, H. Wills.

Sandy: Committed 25 December 1853 for safekeeping by M. Bowman. Released 3 January 1854 to M. Bowman.

Joseph E. ____: Committed 28 December 1853 as a runaway by William Cox.

Released 2 January 1854 to Joseph B. Lece/Lee.

Kitty Franklin: Committed 31 December 1853 as a runaway by James Mosely. Released 9 January 1853 to John Higgins.

Matilda Butler: Committed 4 January 1854 for safekeeping by Charles Kimmel. Released 12 January 1854 to C. Scrivener.

Davy Chimes: Committed 5 January 1854 as a runaway by William Cox. Released 6 January 1854 as a free man.

____ Holland: Committed 6 January 1854 as a runaway by Robert Waters. Released 27 January 1854 to Christopher Brashears.

Edward Pasco: Committed 7 January 1854 as a runaway by Robert T. Malloy. Released 13 January 1854 to Benjamin Padgett.

Kitty: Committed 10 January 1854 for safekeeping by John P. Hilton. Released 12 January 1854 to John P. Hilton.

Jane Levison: Committed 11 January 1854 as a runaway by Isaac Bach. Released 11 January 1854 to George W. Lowery.

Matilda: Committed 7 January 1854 as a runaway by George H. Duvall. Released 13 January 1854 to George W. Young.

Lindsey Wallace: Committed 18 January 1854 as a runaway by George H. Duvall. Released 1 February 1854 to M. Yates.

Savannah Payne: Committed 18 January 1854 as a runaway by James F. Timms. Released

---

[3] This entry was noted as "entered by mistake. Sec. 64".

21 January 1854 to Thomas Marshall.

Louisa: Committed 21 January 1854 for safekeeping by Augusta Ladd. Released 24 January 1854 to Augusta Ladd.

Edward James: Committed 3 February 1854 for safekeeping by Marshall Brown. Released 10 February 1854 to Matthew H. Murray.

Charles Henry Queen: Committed 7 February 1854 as a runaway by Daniel Smith. Released 17 February 1854 to James Spinks.

Washington Smith: Committed 8 February 1854 for safekeeping by J. B. Wilson. Released 13 March 1854 to George Triplett.

Jane Douglass: Committed 10 February 1854 for safekeeping by Louis Mackall. Released 20 February 1854 to B. O. Sheckell.

Jacob Gantt: Committed 11 February 1854 as a runaway by T. C. Donn. Released 20 May 1854 to R. F. Hunt.

William: Committed 13 February 1854 for safekeeping by Michael McDermott. Released 3 April 1854 to J. D. Hoover.

Henry Martin: Committed 14 February 1854 as a runaway by J. W. Beck. Released 23 March 1854 to William O. Drew.

Ignatius Sewell: Committed 15 February 1854 as a runaway by W. A. Malloy. Released 27 February 1854 to J. W. Young.

James Howard: Committed 14 February 1854 as a runaway by R. T. Mills . Released

16 February 1854 to Levi Pumphrey.

John Henry: Committed 3 March 1854 as a runaway by T. C. Donn. Released 6 March 1854 to Gen. George W. Briscoe.

Nancy Hillery: Committed 11 March 1854 as a runaway by T. C. Donn. Released 16 March 1854 to James W. Lowe.

Adam Smith Committed 4 March 1854 as a runaway by T. C. Donn. Released 4 March 1854 to Isaac Scaggs.

Jane Green: Committed 4 March 1854 as a runaway by Isaac Birch. Released 14 March 1854 to B. O. Sheckell.

Marlboro: Committed 3 March 1854 as a runaway by Louis Mackall. Released 4 March 1854 to B. W. Beall.

Jupiter: Committed 3 March 1854 as a runaway by Louis Mackall. Released 4 March 1854 to B. W. Beall.

Tom: Committed 6 March 1854 as a runaway by William Hutchinson. Released 17 March 1854 to Charles S. Middleton.

Margaret: Committed 6 March 1854 as a runaway by William Hutchinson. Released 17 March 1854 to Charles S. Middleton.

Elenora: Committed 6 March 1854 as a runaway by William Hutchinson. Released 17 March 1854 to Charles S. Middleton.

Frank: Committed 8 March 1854 as a runaway by William Hutchinson. Released 14 March 1854 to William Taylor.

Matilda Robinson: Committed 13 March 1854 as a runaway by D. Westerfield. Released

15 March 1854 having proven
her freedom.

Ann and Child Committed
16 March 1854 as a runaway by
Benjamin Fraser. Released
24 March 1854 to Benjamin O.
Sheckell.

Daniel Minor: Committed
16 March 1854 as a runaway by
John Davis. Released 23 March
1854 to J. R. Minor.

John Mortimore: Committed
19 March 1854 for safekeeping
by Hugh Dougherty. Released 3
April 1854.

Ann Jackson: Committed
21 March 1854 as a runaway by
R. T. Mills. Released 2 April
1854 to James Tubman.

Toby Williams: Committed
21 March 1854 as a runaway by
H. T. L. Wilson. Released 2
April 1854 to James Tubman.

John Green: Committed 23 March
1854 as a runaway by William
Cox. Released 24 March 1854
having proven his freedom.

Susanna: Committed 25 March
1854 as a runaway by Samuel
Webster. Released 31 March
1854 to Benjamin O. Sheckell.

Elizabeth Baily: Committed
27 March 1854 as a runaway by
Isaac Birch. Released 1 April
1854 to Benjamin Taylor.

Sarah Williams: Committed
30 March 1854 as a runaway by
Thomas A. Clements. Released
31 March 1854 having proven
her freedom.

Lewis Morris: Committed
30 March 1854 as a runaway by
A. Latruitte. Released 1 April
1854 to Mrs. Richardson.

Mark Coats: Committed 3 April
1854 as a runaway by H.

Ridgeway. Released 8 April
1854 to Mr. Duvall.

Cella Ann Taylor: Committed
3 April 1854 as a runaway by
Isaac Birch. Released 6 April
1854 to Miss E. Miller.

Sandy: Committed 7 April 1854
for safekeeping by John Waters.
Released 18 April 1854 to
Benjamin O. Sheckells.

Lewis Tillman: Committed
10 April 1854 as a runaway by
A. Latruitte. Released 10 April
1854 to William O. Bowie.[4]

Mary Johnson: Committed
19 April 1854 as a runaway by
Isaac Birch. Released 22 April
1854 to Walter F. Brown.

Clarence: Committed 25 April
1854 as a runaway by James W.
Buckley. Released 25 April
1854 to Robert Bowie.

Charles Warren Committed
26 April 1854 as a runaway by
Robert Hurdle. Released
27 April 1854 to Horatio
Clagett.

David Cross: Committed 28 April
1854 as a runaway by A.
Latruitte. Released 2 May 1854
to Richard Williams.

Rebecca: Committed 2 May 1854
for safekeeping by S. C. Busey.
Released 10 May 1854 to
Joseph Simonds.

Walter: Committed 4 May 1854 as
a runaway by Robert N. Lusby.
Released 6 May 1854 to Robert
M. Williams.

Paris Burwell: Committed
8 May 1854 as a runaway by
Wesley Birch. Released 11 May
1854 to Inman Horner.

---

[4] Surname might be Tilghman.

Richard Barnet: Committed
8 May 1854 as a runaway by
Wesley Birch. Released 10 May
1854 to Robert H.
Hunton/Huston.

Nace: Committed 12 May 1854 as
a runaway by R. T. Mills.
Released 13 May 1854 to
Thomas Tolbert.

Nace: Committed 13 May 1854 as
a runaway by Isaac Birch.
Released 14 June 1854 to
Charles Hill.

Fanny Brannan: Committed
11 May 1854 as a runaway by
Isaac Birch. Released 16 May
1854 to B. O. Sheckell.

Sophy: Committed 19 May 1854
for safekeeping by E. E.
O'Brien. Released 16 May 1854
to B. O. Sheckell.

Archey: Committed 20 May 1854
for safekeeping by James Burk.
Released 26 May 1854 to James
Burk.

Cato Crawford: Committed
22 May 1854 as a runaway by
Isaac Birch. Released 29 June
1854 to George W. Beale.

Charlotte & 2 Children:
Committed 22 May 1854 as
runaways by A. Latruitte.
Released 26 May 1854 to
Francis Valdner.

Margaret Barber and child:
Committed 22 May 1854 as
runaways by B. W. Beall.
Released 29 May 1854 to G. M.
Watkins.

Elizabeth: Committed 23 May
1854 for safekeeping by
Thomas C. Magruder. Released
25 May 1854 to J. C. Cook.

Julian: Committed 23 May 1854
for safekeeping by Thomas C.

Magruder. Released 25 May
1854 to J. C. Cook.

Thomas Tilghman: Committed
25 May 1854 as a runaway by
A. Latruitte. Released 29 May
1854 to Mr. Key.

Sarah Green & child: Committed
27 May 1854 as runaways by
H. B. Robertson. Released 3
June 1854 to B. O. Sheckell.

Henry Carroll: Committed 28
May 1854 as a runaway by R.
T. Mills. Released 2 June 1854
to Thomas Clagett.

Rachel & child: Committed
29 May 1854 as runaways by
James W. Allen. Released 3
June 1854 to G. W. Newman.

Daniel: Committed 29 May 1854
as a runaway by Henry Miller.
Released 2 June 1854 to James
Warring.

William Duffin: Committed 5 June
1854 as a runaway by D. Smith.
Released 15 July 1854 to Dr. H.
P. Howard.

Julia Duston: Committed 7 June
1854 for safekeeping by Wesley
O. Stockett. Released 21 June
1854 to Mrs. Simms.

Mary Ann Thomas: Committed
8 June 1854 for safekeeping by
U. S. Marshall. Released 23
June 1854 to Col. H. Naylor.

Celia: Committed 8 June 1854 for
safekeeping by U. S. Marshall.
Released 23 June 1854 to Col.
H. Naylor.

Henry: Committed 8 June 1854 for
safekeeping by U. S. Marshall.
Released 23 June 1854 to Col.
H. Naylor.

John: Committed 8 June 1854 for
safekeeping by U. S. Marshall.
Released 23 June 1854 to Col.
H. Naylor.

Alfred: Committed 11 June 1854 for safekeeping by V. Willet. Released 22 June 1854 to Mr. Harrison.

Susan: Committed 13 June 1854 for safekeeping by Mary Riggs for E. Riggs. Released 24 June 1854 to E. Riggs.

William Watson: Committed 14 June 1854 as a runaway by William Martin. Released 17 June 1854 to Mr. Vermillion.

Dora Simms: Committed 17 June 1854 as a runaway by A. Latruitte. Released 19 June 1854 to David Rawlings.

Jack: Committed 17 June 1854 as a runaway by A. Latruitte. Released to J. M. Krafft 21 June 1854.

Ellen: Committed 19 June 1854 as a runaway by A. E. L. Keese. Released 1 July 1854 to M. H. Litton.

William Murray: Committed 22 June 1854 as a runaway by William Cox. Released 22 June 1854 to Demsey Pagett.

Polly: Committed 23 June 1854 for safekeeping by Henry R. Schoolcraft. Released 30 June 1854 to Benjamin Howard.

Mary Simms: Committed 28 June 1854 for safekeeping by P. W. Browning. Released 29 June 1854 to A. Lee.

Nathaniel: Committed 1 July 1854 as a runaway by Robert Waters. Released 5 July 1854 to C. F. Perry.

Rebecca Ann: Committed 2 July 1854 as a runaway by Robert Waters. Released 6 July 1854 to C. D. Hill.

John: Committed 2 July 1854 as a runaway by R. T. Mills

Released 5 July 1854 to Francis Hall.

Margaret & child: Committed 3 July 1854 as a runaway by Robert Waters. Released 13 July 1854 to J. C. Cook.

Barney: Committed 8 June 1854 for safekeeping by A. Hoover. Released 15 July to J. C. Cook.

Alfred: Committed 11 July 1854 for safekeeping by V. Willett. Released 13 July 1854 to J. C. Cook.

William Colbert: Committed 11 July 1854 as a runaway by Robert Waters. Released 13 July 1854 to Capt. Thos. W. Beard.

James Dorsey: Committed 11 July 1854 as a runaway by William A. Boss. Released 21 July 1854 to C. M. Price.

Amelia: Committed 12 July 1854 as a runaway by Isaac Birch. Released 18 July 1854 to B. O. Sheckell.

Mary Ann Simms: Committed 14 July 1854 for safekeeping by Alexander Lee. Released 15 July 1854 to A. Allen.

Henry Gray: Committed 15 July 1854 as a runaway by Robert Waters. Released 19 July 1854 to Patrick O'Neal.

Richard Bladen: Committed 16 July 1854 as a runaway by James W. Buckley. Released 18 July 1854 to Phillip Edelin.

Sarah Simms: Committed 20 July 1854 as a runaway by J. W. Beck. Released 21 July 1854 to Solomon Herbert.

Jane: Committed 22 July 1854 as a runaway by R. R. Burr. Released 22 July 1854 to B. O. Sheckell.

Thomas: Committed 23 July 1854 as a runaway by J. H. Wise and J. Simonds. Released 23 July 1854 to John A. Frazier.

James: Committed 23 July 1854 as a runaway by J. H. Wise and J. Simonds. Released 23 July 1854 to John A. Frazier.

Sophia: Committed 23 July 1854 as a runaway by J. W. Beck. Released 23 July 1854 to John A. Frazier.

Henry: Committed 24 July 1854 as a runaway by R. R. Burr. Released 26 July 1854 to Alfred M. Berry.

Buck: Committed 27 July 1854 as a runaway by George W. Cissell. Released 27 July 1854 to Benjamin Davis.

William Noland: Committed 27 July 1854 as a runaway by John R. Hoskinson. Released 11 August 1854 to John P. Waring.

Lloyd Gray: Committed 29 July 1854 as a runaway by A. R. Allen. Released 31 July to William Z. Beall.

Pierre Soden: Committed 27 July 1854 as a runaway by H. Thomas. Released 14 September 1854 as a free man.

George Muletta: Committed 27 July 1854 as a runaway by William Cox. Released 10 August 1854 as a free man.

Henry Banks: Committed 11 August 1854 as a runaway by J. W. Kitchen. Released 13 August to Peter Lucas.

David Bell: Committed 8 August 1854 as a runaway by David Westerfield. Released 9 August 1854 as a free man.

Jane: Committed 9 August 1854 for safekeeping by S. C. Busey.

Released 9 August 1854 to Cook & Sheckell.

Emily Barton: Committed 12 August 1854 as a runaway by Isaac Birch. Released 4 September 1854 to Thomas F. Simms.

George Williams: Committed 15 August 1854 as a runaway by U. B. Mitchell. Released 7 September 1854 as a free man.

George Diggs: Committed 15 August 1854 as a runaway by Jeremiah T. Boyden. Released 30 August 1854 to Charles Bowie.

Margaret Barker Committed 16 August 1854 as a runaway by Isaac Birch. Released 19 August 1854 to William M. Watkins.

James Johnson: Committed 18 August 1854 as a runaway by George Hutton. Released 7 September to B. O. Sheckell.

John Brown Committed 21 August 1854 as a runaway by A. Latruitte. Released 30 August 1854. "Not a runaway."

Elvira Diggs: Committed 15 August 1854 as a runaway by William H. Barnachs. Released 25 August 1854 to B. W. Beall.

Samuel Fish: Committed 15 August 1854 as a runaway by A. E. L. Keese. Released 23 August 1854 to John Cruikshanks.

Anthony: Committed 22 August 1854 as a runaway by A. Latruitte. Released 25 August 1854 to George H. Hilleary.

Jenny: Committed 23 August 1854 as a runaway by James

Harrover. Released 30 August
to T. Chesley
Sally: Committed 27 August 1854
as a runaway by John Stewart.
Released 28 September 1854 as
a free woman.
Jacob: Committed 1 September
1854 as a runaway by R. R.
Burr. Released 5 September
1854 to B. J. Jackson.
Elias Triplett: Committed
4 August 1854 as a runaway by
A. E. 1. Keese. Release not
entered. Entry is marked as a
mistake.
Thomas Martin: Committed
5 September 1854 as a runaway
by Charles Kemble. Released 6
September as a free man.
Elizabeth Cottman: Committed
5 September 1854 for
safekeeping by B. W. Beall.
Released 21 September to
Samuel Wise.
Milfred Warren: Committed
5 September 1854 as a runaway
by John Adams. Released 13
September 1854 to
William S. Offut.
Reuben Warren: Committed
5 September 1854 as a runaway
by John Adams. Released 8
September 1854 to John Offut.
Bill: Committed 8 September 1854
for safekeeping by S. J. Little.
Released 13 September 1854 to
S. J. Little.
Joshua Miles: Committed
11 September 1854 as a
runaway by H. T. L. Wilson.
Released 12 September 1854 to
T. E. Kirkley.
Moses Simms: Committed
11 September 1854 as a
runaway by R. R. Burr.

Released 12 September 1854 to
E. Magruder.
Toby: Committed 14 September
1854 as a runaway by Willett
Ridgeway. Released 14
September 1854 to William P.
Pumphrey.
Maria Young: Committed
14 September 1854 as a
runaway by J. F. Wollard.
Released 5 December 1854.
Primus Garner: Committed
15 September 1854 for
safekeeping by J. F. Timms.
Released 23 January 1854 to
H. R. Maryman.
Elizabeth Briscoe: Committed
16 September 1854 as a
runaway by E. G. Handy.
Released 18 October 1854 to
J. H. Southron.
Washington Prater: Committed
22 September 1854 as a
runaway by John Adams.
Released 11 October 1854 to
Charles Anderson.
Nancy: Committed 27 September
1854 for safekeeping by
H. McCormick. Released 27
September 1854 to
H. McCormick.
William Henry Douglass:
Committed 28 September 1854
as a runaway by Washington
Hurley. Released 29 September
1854 as a free man.
Chloe Ann: Committed
30 September 1854 as a
runaway by R. B. Griffin.
Released 10 November 1854 to
Thomas E. Baden.
William Henry alias Tobe:
Committed 3 October 1854 as a
runaway by Levi Hazel.
Released 5 October 1854 to
William P. Pumphrey.

Isaac Marshall: Committed 5 October 1854 as a runaway by William H. Houle. Released 6 October 1854 to Robert Clagett.

William Hamilton: Committed 5 October 1854 as a runaway by A. Latruitte. Released 13 October 1854 to Dr. Grafton Tyler.

Lucinda Somby: Committed 10 October 1854 for safekeeping by S. Douglass. Released 21 June 1855 to T. Sheffer.

Jerry: Committed 15 October 1854 as a runaway by R. T. Mills. Released 26 October 1854 to W. Seaton Belt.

Henry: Committed 15 October 1854 for safekeeping by Charles E. Sherman. Released 18 October 1854 to Charles E. Sherman.

Samuel Stewart: Committed October 1854 as a runaway by A. Latruitte. Released 3 November 1854 to Thomas Javins.

Joe: Committed 5 October 1854 as a runaway by A. Latruitte. Released 23 October 1854 to Phillip Edelin.

Harriet: Committed 5 October 1854 as a runaway by A. Latruitte. Released 20 October 1854. "Not a runaway."

Lewis Bowman: Committed 26 October 1854 as a runaway by James Ward. Released 30 October 1854 to Joseph Young.

William Thomas: Committed 26 October 1854 for safekeeping by Samuel Little. Released 4 November 1854 to B. W. Beall.

Thomas Powell: Committed 26 October 1854 as a runaway by James Ward. Released 30 October 1854 to Dr. G. Tyler.

George Lee: Committed 30 October 1854 as a runaway by William Fanning. Released 1 November 1854 to Joseph Bruin.

Tom: Committed 5 October 1854 as a runaway by A. Latruitte. Released 14 November 1854 to Dr. H. Penn.

Mary Jane Conner: Committed 16 June 1854 for safekeeping by Owen Connelly. Released 8 November 1854 to George Dunlop.

Frank Welden: Committed 8 November 1854 as a runaway by William Rady. Released 10 November 1854 to Robert Bowie.

Spottswood Jackson Faire: Committed 11 November 1854 as a runaway by G. M. Busher. Released 16 November 1854 as a free man.

Ellen: Committed 12 November 1854 as a runaway by John F. Donn. Released 15 November 1854 to Thomas Darnell.

Malinda Harrison: Committed 15 November 1854 as a runaway by A. Latruitte. Released 15 November 1854 to Thomas Scrivener.

Simon: Committed 20 November 1854 for safekeeping by William Stone. Released 29 November 1854 to William Stone.

Henny: Committed 20 November 1854 for safekeeping by William Stone. Released

29 November 1854 to William
Stone.

Nelly: Committed 20 November
1854 for safekeeping by
Grafton Tyler. Released 22
November 1854 to B. W. Beall.

Ellen Godfrey: Committed
8 November 1854 as a runaway
by Bradley Burgess. Released 4
December 1854 as a free
woman.

Daniel Curtis: Committed
20 November 1854 for
safekeeping by William H.
Grinnell. Released 24 January
1854.

Jack: Committed 2 December
1854 as a runaway by Anthony
Latruitte. Released 11
December 1854 to Robert Cruit.

Eveline Brooks: Committed
2 December 1854 as a runaway
by Isaac Stoddard. Released 12
January 1854 as a free woman.

Lewis Joseph Smacum:
Committed 7 December 1854 as
a runaway by J. W. Kitchen.
Released 20 December 1854 to
A. Jones.

Daniel Neale: Committed
8 December 1854 as a runaway
by C. Kemble. Released 4
January 1855 to George Parker.

Frank Digges: Committed
22 December 1854 as a
runaway by R. R. Burr.
Released 23 December 1854 to
Thomas Perkins.

Adela Genery: Committed
26 December 1854 as a
runaway by Anthony Latruitte.
Released 23 December 1854 to
R. F. Isaacs.

Lewis: Committed 26 December
1854 as a runaway by T. A.
Talbert & W. Shelton. Released

2 January 1855 to James E.
Gwynn.

Frank: Committed 28 December
1854 as a runaway by James S.
Buckley. Released 2 January
1855 to John Gwynn.

Vincent: Committed 28 December
1854 as a runaway by James S.
Buckley. Released 2 January
1855 to John Gwynn.

Sandy: Committed 29 December
1854 as a runaway by Anthony
Latruitte. Released 13 January
1855 to Gustavus White.

John: Committed 30 December
1854 for safekeeping by
Charles Werner. Released
1 January 1855.

Charles Gordon: Committed
22 January 1855 for
safekeeping Released
1 February 1855 to
Fielder Darnall.

Lucy: Committed 3 January 1855
for safekeeping by Dr. Mackall.
Released 5 January 1855.

Martha: Committed 4 January
1855 for safekeeping by Clark
Mills. Released 8 January 1855
to Clark Mills.

Davis Walker: Committed
6 January 1855 for safekeeping
by I. Y. Smoot. Released 8
January 1855 to I. Y. Smoot.

William Woodland: Committed
6 January 1855 as a runaway by
James S. Buckley. Released 9
January 1855 to Thomas B. Sly.

Frank Bowen: Committed
10 January 1855 for
safekeeping by John Waters.
Released 20 January 1855 to
John Waters.

Theodore: Committed 30 January
1855 for safekeeping by
Solomon Stover. Released 26

January 1855 to Solomon
Stover.

Emily & child: Committed
6 January 1855 for safekeeping
by George T. Massey, agent.
Released 1 February 1855 to
William Cox.

Tom: Committed 26 January 1855
for safekeeping by James J.
Forbes. Released 6 March 1855
to James J. Forbes.

John Bird: Committed 26 January
1855 for safekeeping by
William Cox. Released 14
February 1855 to William Cox.

Caroline: Committed 4 February
1855 as a runaway by Thomas
Brightwell. Released
12 February 1855 to John H.
Gwynn.

Gracy: Committed 10 February
1855 for safekeeping by A. B.
Berry. Released 18 February
1855 to Thomas J. Massie.

Mary Bud: Committed
14 February 1855 for
safekeeping by William M.
Moore. Released 14 February
1855 to William M. Moore.

Josephine: Committed
14 February 1855 for
safekeeping by Michael
McDermott. Released 19
February to Michael
McDermott.

Lewis Diggs: Committed
17 February 1855 by Daniel
Smith as a runaway. Released
21 February 1855 to William
Offut.

Frank: Committed 18 February
1855 by James Ward as a
runaway. Released 8 March
1855 to S. C. Wroe.

Sam Carroll: Committed
22 February 1855 by A. R.

Allen as a runaway. Released
24 February 1855 to
Zach B. Beall.

Ben: Committed 23 February 1855
by R. T. Mills as a runaway.
Released 28 February 1855 to
Mordecai Mitchell.

Harriet: Committed 24 February
1855 by A. Latruitte as a
runaway. Released 1 March
1855 to H. McCeny.

Ben: Committed 24 February 1855
by A. Latruitte as a runaway.
Released 26 February 1855 to
John Hoover.

Gracy: Committed 3 March 1855
for safekeeping by A. B. Berry.
Released 20 April 1855 to A. B.
Berry.

John Deveal: Committed
16 March 1855 by J. W.
Kitchen as a runaway. Released
12 April 1855 to J. Spinks.

Thomas Sprigg: Committed
25 March 1855 by J. W.
Kitchen as a runaway. Release
not recorded.

Richard Tilghman: Committed
16 March 1855 by J. W.
Kitchen as a runaway. Release
not recorded.

Elbert Baker: Committed
28 March 1855 by James Ward
as a runaway. Released 21 April
1855 to Robert L. Teale.

Jefferson: Committed 31 March
1855 by R. T. Mills as a
runaway. Released 21 April
1855 to G. W. Newman.

Henry Gibbs: Committed as a
runaway by R. Waters 4 April
1855. Released 14 May 1855 to
George Peters.

Sarah Washington: Committed as
a runaway by John H. Taylor

9 April 1855. Released 11 April 1855 to Robert Darnes.

Saulsbury Brooks: Committed as a runaway by A. Latruitte. Released 6 April 1855 to Dr. Sothoron.

Isaac: Committed 10 April 1855 for safekeeping by James H. Birch. Released 12 April 1855 to James Spinks.

Jacob French: Committed as a runaway by B. W. Beall 12 April 1855. Released 11 may 1855 to John A. Grimes.

Phillip: Committed 10 April 1855 for safekeeping by John Contee. Released 25 April 1855 to John Contee.

Primus Garner: Committed 10 April 1855 for safekeeping by James Fowler. Released 20 June 1855 to James Fowler.

John: Committed as a runaway by R. Waters 16 April 1855. Released 18 April 1855 to Mr. Duckett.

Eliza Carroll: Committed as a runaway by William Cox 16 April 1855. Released 16 June 1855 to James Ward.

John Brown: Committed 20 April 1855 for safekeeping by James Edelin. Released 22 April 1855 to Pompey.

Henry: Committed 25 April 1855 for safekeeping by James Maher. Released 11 May 1855 to James Maher.

Molly: Committed 28 April 1855 for safekeeping by H. W. Blunt. Released 1 May 1855 to H. W. Blunt.

Lewis Thompson: Committed as a runaway by James S. Buckley 2 May 1855. Released 5 May 1855 to Susannah Mudd.

Richard Ennis: Committed as a runaway by J. F. Stewart 4 May 1855. Released 5 May 1855 as a free man.

Rosanna Gordon: Committed as a runaway by B. W. Beall. Released 6 May 1855 to A. R. Allen.

Catherine & child: Committed 5 May 1855 for safekeeping by A. B. Berry. Released 15 May 1855 to A. B. Berry.

Henry: Committed as a runaway by Leonard Reeves 6 May 1855. Released 8 May 1855 to R. L. Smallwood.

Daniel Hall: Committed 10 May 1855 for safekeeping by George McCeney. Released 12 May 1855 to James H. Birch.

Celina Walker: Committed as a runaway by R. Waters 8 May 1855. Released 8 May 1855 to John Young.

Rosetta Davis: Committed 9 May 1855 for safekeeping by W. A. Mulloy. Released 17 May 1855 to Henderson Fowler.

Washington Stuart: Committed as a runaway by J. F. Wollard 15 May 1855. Released 17 May 1855 to Benjamin Walker.

William Johnson: Committed 22 May 1855 as a runaway by George A. Brest. Released 26 May 1855 as a free man.

Rufus Jackson: Committed 11 June 1855 as a runaway by H. Thomas. Released 12 June 1855 to William H. Benson.

Thomas: Committed 12 June 1855 as a runaway by J. F. Timms. Released 20 June 1855 to John W. Anderson.

Benjamin Frederick Committed 15 June 1855 as a runaway by

S. S. Nowland. Released 18 June 1855 to Dr. Brown.

Eliza: Committed 16 June 1855 for safekeeping by H. Longborough. Released 13 July 1855 to H. Longborough.

Butler: Committed 17 June 1855 as a runaway by John McNamara. Released 20 June 1855 to John Serratt.

John: Committed 20 June 1855 as a runaway by Charles Kemble. Released 24 June 1855 to E. B. Butlard.

Mark: Committed 25 June 1855 as a runaway by R. R. Burr. Released 27 July 1855 to Dr. Duvall.

John: Committed 30 June 1855 for safekeeping by Edward H. Edelin. Released 9 July 1855 to Edward H. Edelin.

Robert Brown: Committed 3 July 1855 as a runaway by A. E. L. Keese. Released 19 November 1855 as a free man.

Eliza Fletcher: Committed 4 July 1855 as a runaway by Isaac Stoddard. Released 5 July 1855 to "Roberts".

Mary Young: Committed 5 July 1855 as a runaway by A. Latruitte. Released 13 July to D. Smith.

Richard: Committed 9 July 1855 as a runaway by William Hutcherson. Released 16 July 1855 to Mr. Downing.

Henry Hill: Committed 5 June 1855 for safekeeping by James Maher. Released 7 July 1855 to James Maher.

Grandville Williams: Committed 13 July 1855 as a runaway by Henry Thomas. Released 25 July 1855 as a free man.

Isaac Jones: Committed 13 July 1855 as a runaway by Robert Waters. Released 14 July 1855 to Mr. Berry.

Susan King: Committed 14 July 1855 as a runaway by A. R. Allen. Release not recorded.

Maria Brent: Committed 23 July 1855 as a runaway by Robert Waters. Released 23 July 1855 to Mr. Hunter.

Nace Hodge: Committed 25 July 1855 as a runaway by Robert Waters. Released 16 August 1855 to Thomas Bell.

Mathew: Committed 27 July 1855 as a runaway by R. T. Mills. Released 4 September 1855 to John H. Duckett.

Mary & two children: Committed 16 June 1855 for safekeeping by John Little. Released 31 July 1855 to Mr. Cook.

Hilley Wallace: Committed 28 July 1855 as a runaway by Robert Waters. Released 28 July 1855 to Robert Dick.

Lewis Jones: Committed 30 July 1855 as a runaway by Robert Waters. Released 18 August 1855 to Zedock Sasseer.

William Hackey: Committed 30 July 1855 as a runaway by D. Westerfield. Released 31 July 1855 as a free man.

William H. Summerville: Committed 31 July 1855 as a runaway by Robert Bayliss. Released 22 September 1855 to Samuel Strong.

Isaac White: Committed 1 August 1855 as a runaway by William Cox. Released 6 October 1855 as a free man.

George White: Committed 1 August 1855 for safekeeping

by Mary E. D. Waugh.
Released 10 August 1855 to
Mary E. D. Waugh.

William: Committed 1 August
1855 as a runaway by R. R.
Burr. Released 21 August
12855 to Dr. James Mulligan.

Richard Tyler: Committed
12 August 1855 as a runaway
by David Hanover. Released 30
August 1855 as a free man.

Rufus: Committed 3 August 1855
as a runaway by John O. Harry.
Released 6 August 1855 to
William Benson.

John Wilson: Committed 3 August
1855 as a runaway by William
Cox. Released 26 March 1856
as a free man.

Henry Crumpton: Committed
4 August 1855 as a runaway by
A. Latruitte. Released 4 August
1855 to Dr. Mackall.

Robert Fletcher: Committed
28 July 1855 as a runaway by
R. S. Mills. Released 1 August
1855 to John Berry.

Leano and two children:
Committed 10 August 1855 for
safekeeping by H. Corcoran.
Released 17 August to E. G.
Handy.

Julia Snowden: Committed
16 August 1855 as a runaway
by Charles Kemble. Released
24 August 1855 to Mr. Price.

William Taylor: Committed
16 August 1855 for safekeeping
by Mrs. P. Gadsby. Released 21
August 1855 to Wi;;iam Cox.

Davy: Committed 17 August 1855
as a runaway by J. A. Willet.
Released 29 August 1855 to
Nathaniel Soper.

Charles: Committed 17 August
1855 as a runaway by Norwood

and Stewart. Released
24 August 1855 to S. B. Moore.

Lloyd Mason: Committed
18 August 1855 for safekeeping
by A. E. L. Keese. Released
21 August to A. E. L. Keese.

Sophy: Committed 21 August 1855
for safekeeping by E. E.
O'Brian. Released 1 September
1855 to Levi Pumphrey.

Kitty Franklin: Committed
22 August 1855 as a runaway
by W. Barnes. Released
28 August 1855 to
John Higgins.

Lloyd Mason: Committed
22 August 1855 for safekeeping
by A. E. L. Keese. Released to
H. B. Sweeny.

Abraham: Committed 22 August
1855 for safekeeping by A. E.
L. Keese. Released to John E.
Robey 30 August 1855.

William Taylor: Committed
22 August 1855 for safekeeping
by A. E. L. Keese. Released to
"servant man Joshua" 25
August 1855.

Julia: Committed 22 August 1855
as a runaway by R. H. Tunnell.
Released 6 September 1855 to
R. H. Tunnell.

John Contee: Committed
3 September 1855 as a runaway
by R. H. Tunnell. Released 6
September 1855 to
R. H. Tunnell.

Henny: Committed 4 September
1855 for safekeeping by V.
Willett. Released 12 September
1855 by V. Willett.

Nelly Brown alias Letty Diggs:
Committed 4 September 1855
as a runaway by J. S. Norwood.
Released 2 October 1855 to
Samuel C. Wroe.

Patsy Brown Committed
7 September 1855 as a runaway
by Yeatman and Wilson.
Released 14 September 1855 to
Henry Dangerfield.

Caroline Bush: Committed
8 September 1855 as a runaway
by John Little. Released
15 September 1855 to Mr. Ball.

Washington Greenleaf:
Committed 9 September 1855
as a runaway by E. Y. Handy.
Released 11 September 1855 to
Basil Brown.

Joseph: Committed 10 September
1855 for safekeeping by Lewis
Coruse. Released 17 September
1855 to Lewis Coruse.

Caroline Parker and Susan:
Committed 10 September 1855
for safekeeping by J. B. Boone.
Released 22 September to
Bowling and Thomas.

William Herbert: Committed
11 September 1855 for
safekeeping by W. Rawlings.
Released 11 September 1855 to
Joseph Mead.

Henry Proctor: Committed
11 September 1855 as a
runaway by Robert Waters.
Released 5 October 1855 to
Sallie Connelly.

Sandy Hawkins: Committed
12 September 1855 for
safekeeping by William
Matthews. Released 15 October
1855 to Mr. Spinks.

Henry Marlow: Committed
15 September 1855 for
safekeeping by W. O. Drew.
Released 16 September 1855 to
W. O. Drew.

Joe Brown: Committed
17 September 1855 for
safekeeping by Francis Brent.

Released 18 September 1855 to
Robert S. Chilton.

Hilley Lemons: Committed
4 September 1855 as a runaway
by A. LaTruitte. Released
8 October 1855 to L. Morton.

Ann Fenwick: Committed
25 September 1855 as a
runaway by R. R. Burr.
Released 29 November 1855 to
J. R. Brent.

James: Committed 25 September
1855 as a runaway by Robert
Waters. Released 19 October
1855 to John E. Berry.

Harriette: Committed
28 September 1855 as a
runaway by John Lear.
Released 2 October 1855 to
Mary Lear.

Caroline: Committed
28 September 1855 for
safekeeping by M. H. Thomas.
Released 29 September 1855 to
General Gosman.

Angaline: Committed
29 September 1855 for
safekeeping by R. E.
Thompson. Released
10 October 1855 to R. E.
Thompson.

Thomas Anderson: Committed
30 September 1855 as a
runaway by R. R. Burr.
Released 30 September 1855 to
A. W. Russell.

Richard Dorsey: Committed
30 September 1855 as a
runaway by R. R. Burr.
Released 1 October 1855 to
Mr. Lumbson.

William Dorsey: Committed
30 September 1855 as a
runaway by R. R. Burr.
Released 30 September 1855 to
Mr. Bradley.

Daniel: Committed 30 September 1855 as a runaway by R. R. Burr. Released 16 October 1855 to B. Hall.

Jacob: Committed 2 October 1855 as a runaway by Cop and Parham. Released 6 October 1855 to M. H. Vincent.

John Hardin: Committed 6 October 1855 as a runaway by James Ward. Released 19 October 1855 to Henry C. McCeney.

Elbert Baker: Committed 6 October 1855 as a runaway by James Ward. Released 11 October 1855 to J. E. Robey.

John Brown: Committed 6 October 1855 for safekeeping by J. W. Kitchen. Released 11 October 1855 to Mr. Daniel.

William Sprigg: Committed 6 October 1855 as a runaway by John Bayley. Released 22 October 1855 to Samuel Birch.

Thomas Saunders: Committed 10 October 1855 as a runaway by John E. Bailey. Released 11 October 1855 to C. W. Alexander.

Sam: Committed 13 October 1855 for safekeeping by John Harry. Released 25 November 1855 to John E. Robey.

N. Francis Ford: Committed 14 October 1855 as a runaway by J. W. Kitchens. Released 17 October 1855 to Thomas C. Magruder.

Henny & two children: Committed 19 October 1855 for safekeeping by Thomas R. Bird. Released 16 November 1855 to Thomas R. Bird.

Jane & child: Committed 31 October 1855 for safekeeping by Willet. Released 15 November 1855 to John Gammel.

Bill: Committed 1 November 1855 for safekeeping by A. E. L. Keese. Released 3 November 1855 to A. E. L. Keese.

Fanny E. Brooks: Committed 1 November 1855 for safekeeping by Anthony Smith. Released 2 November 1855 to A. Hyde.

Robert: Committed 2 November 1855 for safekeeping by William D. Bell. Released 5 November 1855 to W. D. Bell.

Louisa Johnson: Committed 2 November 1855 for safekeeping by A. E. L. Keese. Released 5 November 1855 to A. E. L. Keese.

Alexander Long: Committed 4 November 1855 as a runaway by John Davis. Released 6 November 1855 to W. Lynham.

Ben McCubbin: Committed 5 November 1855 as a runaway by A. LaTruitte. Released 13 November 1855 to Benjamin Bohrer.

Daniel: Committed 6 November 1855 as a runaway by Willet. Released 10 November 1855 to William B. Hill.

Margaret Smith & child: Committed 8 November 1855 as a runaway by James H. Birch. Released 10 November 1855 S. J. Thompson.

William Taylor: Committed 9 November 1855 for safekeeping by W. Cox. Released 10 November 1855 to William Cox.

Sam: Committed 10 November 1855 as a runaway by R. T.

Mills. Released 16 November 1855 to Charles C. Hill.

Joseph Simms: Committed 13 November 1855 as a runaway by William A. Malloy. Released 4 December 1855 to George W. Young.

Kajer: Committed 17 November 1855 as a runaway by Francis Ward. Released 24 November 1855 to Addison Bett.

John H. Williams: Committed 23 November 1855 as a runaway by Isaac Stoddard. Released 24 November 1855 to Dr. Gunnell.

Arianna Hawley: Committed 26 November 1855 as a runaway by A. LaTruitte. Released 27 November 1855 to Mr. Spinks.

George: Committed 26 November 1855 for safekeeping by Frank T. Grady. Released 27 November 1855 to Wes Cox.

George Simms: Committed 28 November 1855 as a runaway by A. R. Allen. Released 30 November 1855 to John B. Hereford.

John Randolph: Committed 30 November 1855 as a runaway by W. S. Hurley. Released 6 December 1855 to Sampson Jones.

Beck: Committed 2 December 1855 for safekeeping by William Y. Busey. Released 19 December 1855 to J. W. Burroughs.

Charles Fletcher: Committed 2 December 1855 as a runaway by A. LaTruitte. Released 6 December 1855 to A. B. Berry.

Susan & child: Committed 8 December 1855 as a runaway by William Cox. Released 13 December 1855 as a free woman.

Rose: Committed 15 December 1855 for safekeeping by W. G. Swann. Released 27 December 1855 to W. T. Swann.

Mary Jackson & child: Committed 18 December 1855 as a runaway by James Ward. Released 18 December 1855 to Robert K. Nevitt.

Reuben Blair: Committed 19 December 1855 as a runaway by A. LaTruitte. Released 9 January 1855 to Henry Bradly.

Daniel Weldon: Committed 19 December 1855 as a runaway by A. LaTruitte. Released 22 December 1855 to W. S. Wilson.

Maurice: Committed 19 December 1855 as a runaway by John Davis. Released 20 February 1855 to Robert Dunlop.

George: Committed 21 December 1855 for safekeeping by Judson Naylor. Released 28 December 1855 to Judson Naylor.

Pheby: Committed 28 December 1855 for safekeeping by James Tally. Released 29 December 1855 to James Tally.

Joe: Committed 28 December 1855 for safekeeping by James Tally. Released 29 December 1855 to James Tally.

John: Committed 2 January 1856 as a runaway by John Hodgkin. Released 15 January 1856 to R. C. Brooke.

Henry Bowen: Committed 6 January 1856 as a runaway by William Cox. Released 15 January 1856 to Richard Cissel.

Harriet Newton: Committed 8 January 1856 as a runaway by A. Latruitte. Released 8 January 1856 to Dr. DuHamel.

Henry Barnes: Committed 8 January 1856 as a runaway by A. Latruitte. Released 8 January 1856 to George W. Hardesty.

Ann Johnson: Committed 11 January 1856 as a runaway by A. R. Allen. Released 12 January 1856 to ___ Wheeler.

John: Committed 16 January 1856 for safekeeping by E. Y. Handy. Released 25 January 1856 to L. Winters.

James Stanmore: Committed 16 January 1856 as a runaway by Baley Brown. Released 22 January to Dr. W. Peach.

David Slater: Committed 16 January 1856 as a runaway by John Mozine. Released 24 January 1856 to James S. Morsell.

Samuel Slater: Committed 16 January 1856 as a runaway by John Mozine. Released 24 January 1856 to James S. Morsell.

William Griffith: Committed 16 January 1856 as a runaway by John Mozine. Released 24 January 1856 to James S. Morsell.

Lethe Diggs: Committed 18 January 1856 for safekeeping by Louis Lepress. Released 17 March 1856 to Louis Lepress.

Robert Brown: Committed 19 January 1856 as a runaway by John O'Harry. Released 29 January 1856 to A. E. H. Darne.

John: Committed 3 January 1856 for safekeeping by W. Nailor

for Allison Nailor. Released 7 January 1856 to M. J. Carper.

Walter Humphreys: Committed 28 January 1856 as a runaway by John H. Wise. Released 30 January 1856 to Francis Kirby.

Albert Hickman: Committed 28 January 1856 as a runaway by E. O. Sanderson. Released 29 January 1856 to N. Marshall.

George: Committed 30 January 1856 for safekeeping by W. Herron. Released 6 February 1856 to W. T. Herron.

Richard: Committed 31 January 1856 as a runaway by Robert T. Mills. Released 20 February 1856 to William N. Bowie.

Laura: Committed 2 February 1856 as a runaway by Robert Mills. Released 20 February 1856 to George W. Newman.

Ellen Gould: Committed 4 February 1856 as a runaway by James Ward. Released 9 February 1856 to William Duckett.

Henry Chase: Committed 5 February 1856 for safekeeping by H. Yeatman. Released 5 February 1856 to W. W. Hays.

Jane: Committed 6 February 1856 for safekeeping by E. M. Chapin. Released 7 February 1856 to E. M. Chapin.

Jacob Coates: Committed 11 February 1856 as a runaway by Benjamin Padget. Released 3 March 1856 to J. E. Robey.

Joseph Simms: Committed 22 February 1856 as a runaway by James S. Buckley. Released 3 March 1856 to J. E. Robey.

Julia Duvall: Committed 26 February 1856 as a runaway

by A. LaTruitte. Released
8 March 1856 to Dr. James
Wallace.

Lewis Miles: Committed
27 February 1856 as a runaway
by W. T. Burdett. Released
8 March 1856 to N. M. Lee.

Maria Baker: Committed
28 February 1856 for
safekeeping by John B. Boone.
Released 29 February 1856 to J.
S. Robey.

Lucy & Otho: Committed 6 March
1856 for safekeeping by N. M.
Lee. Released 8 March 1856 to
N. M. Lee.

Ben Cury: Committed 7 March
1856 for safekeeping by Isaac
Foulke. Released 10 March
1856 to Isaac Fouke.

Daniel: Committed 8 March 1856
for safekeeping by John E.
Robey. Released 12 March
1856 to John E. Robey.

Stephen: Committed 10 March
1856 for safekeeping by John
A. Cassell. Released 15 March
1856 to John A. Cassell.

Richard Marshall: Committed
10 March 1856 for safekeeping
by Z. K. Offut. Released 12
March 1856 to Joseph S.
Worthington.

Joseph: Committed 22 March 1856
for safekeeping by Zack B.
Brooke. Released 23 March
1856 to Z. B. Brooke.

Charles Carroll: Committed
22 March 1856 as a runaway by
Phillip Otterback Jr. Released
29 March 1856 to Richard H.
Taylor.

Edward: Committed 27 March
1856 for safekeeping by
William Cox. Released 24 April
1856 to Richard Wallach.

Jerry Gordon: Committed
28 March 1856 for safekeeping
by G. W. Young. Released
31March 1856 to G. W. Young.

George: Committed 31 March
1856 for safekeeping by John
A. Smith. Released 19 April
1856 to John A. Smith.

Henry: Committed 31 March 1856
for safekeeping by John A.
Smith. Released 19 April 1856
to John A. Smith.

Romeo: Committed 8 April 1856
as a runaway by Robert Waters.
Released 8 April 1856 to J. B.
Hereford.

Luke Carter: Committed 10 April
1856 as a runaway by James
Waters. Released 19 April 1856
to R. Sheckells.

Henry Davis: Committed 14 April
1856 as a runaway by Robert
Waters. Released 22 April 1856
to D. Smith.

John Chapel: Committed 15 April
1856 as a runaway by James A.
Williams. Released 22 April
1856 to John A. Barber.

Lizzie: Committed 17 April 1856
for safekeeping by Mr. Pigott.
Released 18 April 1856 to
William.

John Fletcher: Committed
17 April 1856 as a runaway by
Robert Mills. Released 18 April
to Charles C. Hill.

Thomas Shorter: Committed
17 April 1856 as a runaway by
Robert Mills. Released 18 April
to Charles C. Hill.

Robert Fletcher: Committed
17 April 1856 as a runaway by
Robert Mills. Released 18 April
to Charles C. Hill.

Jack Butter: Committed 21 April
1856 for safekeeping by W. D.

Bell. Released 21 April 1856 to W. D. Dell.

Joseph Campbell: Committed 23 April 1856 as a runaway by John Rogers. Released 29 April 1856 to H. A. Middleton.

Nace Gross: Committed 23 April 1856 as a runaway by Robert Waters. Released 29 April 1856 to John Bowie.

Sandy Jackson: Committed 24 April 1856 for safekeeping by William Z. Beall. Released 4 May 1856 to John E. Robey.

Phillip Barbour: Committed 26 April 1856 as a runaway by W. A. Boss. Released 2 May 1856 to W. A. Boss.

John Bell: Committed 27 April 1856 as a runaway by Robert Waters. Released 2 May 1856 to M. Clagett.

Arthur Alexander: Committed 28 April 1856 as a runaway by C. G. Echloff. Released 21 May 1856 as free.

Francis Smith: Committed 2 May 1856 as a runaway by A. LaTruitte. Released 5 May 1856 to Jane E. Johns.

Ben: Committed 24 April 1856 for safekeeping by A. B. Berry. Released 15 May 1856 to A. B. Berry.

Pompy: Committed 12 May 1856 as a runaway by E. H. Edelin. Released 11 May 1856 to E. H. Edelin.

John Burnet: Committed 7 May 1856 as a runaway by A. E. L. Reese. Released 17 May 1856 to Dr. R. S. Patterson.

William: Committed 12 May 1856 as a runaway by John Rogers. Released 15 May 1856 to J. W. Brown.

Elizabeth Dodson: Committed 13 May 1856 as a runaway by Stoddard & Mitchell. Released 15 May 1856 to George Johnson.

Henry Williams: Committed 14 May 1856 as a runaway by J. W. Kitchen. Released 16 May 1856 to Mrs. Middleton.

Simon: Committed 17 May 1856 as a runaway by Dr. B. King. Released 6 June 1856 to Mr. Wahl.

Etta Robinson: Committed 18 May 1856 for safekeeping by W. D. Bell. Released 19 May 1856 to A. Russell.

Howard Freeman: Committed 19 May 1856 as a runaway by U. B. Mitchell. Released 29 May 1856 as free.

Ann Boarman: Committed 21 May 1856 as a runaway by W. A. Boss. Released 16 June 1856 to N. F. Blacklock.

Sylvester Boarman: Committed 17 May 1856 as a runaway by W. A. Boss. Released 16 June 1856 to N. F. Blacklock.

Sandy Green: Committed 8 June 1856 as a runaway by Robert Mills. Released 11 June 1856. (no other notation).

Jerry Jenifer: Committed 10 June 1856 as a runaway by J. F. Simms. Released 16 June 1856 to B. O. Sheckells.

Henry Lucas: Committed 12 June 1856 as a runaway by J. F. King. Released 24 June 1856 to Miss A. Gray.

Sarah J. Beckman: Committed 15 June 1856 as a runaway by R. H. Trunnell. Released 15 June 1856 as free.

Ann M. Bulger: Committed 21 July 1856 as a runaway by A. LaTruitte. Released 23 July 1856 to J. C. Cooke.

R. H. Gallaher. Released 3 August 1856 to J. H. Weller.

Frank: Committed 17 June 1856 as a runaway by G. W. Richardson. Only release note omits date and states "Taken out by Mulligan".

Margaret Johnson: Committed 15 June 1856 as a runaway by J. F. King. Released 11 October 1856 as free.

Thomas Smith: Committed 20 June 1856 as a runaway by J. W. Reynolds. Released 4 October 1856 to _____ Middleton.

Mary A. World: Committed 20 June 1856 as a runaway by A. R. Allen. Released 21 June 1856 as free.

Charles Carroll: Committed 23 June 1856 for safekeeping by R. B. Hughes. Released 30 June 1856 to R. B. Hughes.

Ann Mills: Committed 24 June 1856 for safekeeping by John Wiley. Released 25 June 1856 to 'Sheckels'.

Emily Mills: Committed 24 June 1856 for safekeeping by John Wiley. Released 4 July 1856 to John Wiley.

John Addison: Committed 25 June 1856 for safekeeping by F. Soffell. Released 8 July 1856 to J. C. Robey.

William Hall: Committed 25 June 1856 as a runaway by Robert Mills. Released 28 June to Mr. Morris.

Richard Hanson: Committed 26 June 1856 as a runaway by J. S.

Norwood. Released 25 July 1856 to James J. Pumphrey.

Catherine Williams: Committed 25 June 1856 as a runaway by J. W. Kitchens. Released January 30 1857 as free.

George Black[5]: Committed 3 July 1856 as a runaway by William Johnson. Released as a free man 5 July 1856.

Daniel Batson: Committed 3 July 1856 as a runaway by Joseph Gill. Released 7 July 1856 as a free man.

Edward Appleton: Committed 6 July 1856 as a runaway by James Ward. Released 15 July 1856. No person noted.

John Bailey: Committed 12 July 1856 as a runaway by J. Gittings. Released 15 July 1856. No person noted.

Charity Edwards: Committed 16 July 1856 as a runaway by Robert Waters. Released 21 July 1856. No person noted.

Washington Onley: Committed 17 July 1856 as a runaway by Francis Reilly. Released 15 July 1856 to N. Howard.

Rosan Gordon: Committed 18 July 1856 as a runaway by Francis Reilly. Released 15 July 1856 to Mary Hall.

Rufus: Committed 18 July 1856 as a runaway by W. H. Barnacloe. Released 22 July 1856 to Dr. Scoot. (Scot?).

James Robinson : Committed 27 July 1856 as a runaway by Daniel Rodstein. Released 21 July 1856 to Jacob Hines.

---

[5] The Surname 'Black' is crossed out in the original.

Richard Thompson: Committed 21 July 1856 as a runaway by A. LaTruitte. Released 23 July 1856 to J. C. Cooke.

Lloyd Thompson: Committed 21 July 1856 as a runaway by A. LaTruitte. Released 23 July 1856 to J. C. Cooke.

Letha Gordon: Committed 21 July 1856 as a runaway by A. LaTruitte. Released 23 July 1856 to J. C. Cooke.

Dora Simms: Committed 23 July 1856 as a runaway by Robert Waters. Released 24 July 1856.

Jesse Curtis: Committed 24 July 1856 as a runaway by A. R. Allen & W. Boss. Released 27 July 1856 to Robert Peaters.

Pomp: Committed 18 May 1856 for safekeeping by R. Poole. Released 28 July 1856 to Perry LaTrundle.

Isaac: Committed 18 May 1856 for safekeeping by Perry La Trundle. Released 26 July 1856 to W. Cook.

Harry Hadden: Committed 26 July 1856 as a runaway by James Ennis. Released 28 July 1856 to Henry.

Frank Cover: Committed 28 May 1856 for safekeeping by C. Alexander. Released 22 September 1856 to Samuel _____.

Eliza Stewart: Committed 28 July 1856 as a runaway by Y. H. Langley. Released 29 July 1856 to S. Scaggs.

Martha Brown: Committed 29 July 1856 as a runaway by Robert Waters. Released 27 August 1856 to Dr. Waters.

Hester Brown: Committed 29 July 1856 as a runaway by Robert Waters. Released 27 August 1856 to Dr. Waters.

James Iram: Committed 29 July 1856 as a runaway by J. W. Reynolds. Released 28 August 1856 to John E. Berry.

Lewis: Committed 30 July 1856 as a runaway by Robert Waters. Released 2 August 1856 to Clagett.

William Alfred: Committed 1 August 1856 for safekeeping by E. H. Edelin. Released 6 August 1856 to W. Sheekells.

Frank, Nora, Lilley, and Lewisa: Committed 3 August 1856 for safekeeping by John T. W. Dean. Released 6 August 1856 to John T. W. Dean.

Caroline Howard: Committed 3 August 1856 as a runaway by D. A. Harriover. Released 8 August 1856 to Charles Bowie.

Samuel Clagget: Committed 6 August 1856 for safekeeping H. B. Sweeney. Released 15 August 1856 to H. B. Sweeney.

Hilery Young: Committed 6 August 1856 for safekeeping by H. B. Sweeney. Released 6 September 1856 to J. C. Cooke.

Lewellen Williams: Committed 12 August 1856 as a runaway by James Gipson. Released 31 August 1856 to W. A. Waugh.

Sylvester Brooks: Committed 13 August 1856 as a runaway by John W. Rogers. Released 16 August 1856 to Mrs. Sanders.

Charles Jones alias W. Green: Committed 15 August 1856 as a runaway by W. A. Boss.

Released 18 August 1856 as a free man.

John T. Bowers: Committed 17 August 1856 as a runaway by Robert Mills. Released 21 August 1856.

John H. Tiles: Committed 17 August 1856 as a runaway by Robert Mills. Released 18 August 1856 to Darnell.

Thomas Henry Slater: Committed 18 August 1856 as a runaway by James Ennis. Released 19 August 1856.

Emeline Shaw: Committed 19 August 1856 as a runaway by E. B. Devall. Released 22 August 1856 to James W. Birch.

George Wright alias Black Hawk: Committed 25 August 1856 as a runaway by Captain Horseman. Released 1 8 September 1856 as free.

Henry: Committed 26 August 1856 as a runaway by Leonard Reeves. Released 30 August 1856 to Alfred Gardner.

James Chase: Committed 15 August 1856 as a runaway by Joseph B. Claget for A. LaTruitte. Released 22 September 1856 to Mr. Cook.

Nace Tabbs: Committed 1 September 1856 as a runaway by Robert Mills. Released 3 September 1856 to R. N. Darnell.

Margrat: Committed 15 September 1856 as a runaway by R. R. Burr. Released 17 September 1856 to Robert Taylor.

William Agee: Committed 18 September 1856 as a runaway by W. L. Ross. Released 19 September 1856 to Mr. Appick.

Lewis B___: Committed 19 September 1856 as a runaway by J. Cooper. Released 22 September 1856 to Mr. Price.

Albert Jones: Committed 19 September 1856 as a runaway by J. Cooper. Released 19 September 1856 as free.

Edward Graham: Committed 19 September 1856 for safekeeping by G. W. Young. Released 22 September 1856 to G. W. Young.

Margaret Humpres: Committed 6 August 1856 as a fugitive. Died in jail.

Lyla Knowles: Committed 19 September 1856 as a runaway by John Rogers. Released 24 September 1856 to J. B. Baleh.

Thomas Aver: Committed 3 September 1856 for safekeeping by Pulizze. Released 3 September 1856 to Pulizze.

Emanuel alias John Parker: Committed 28 September 1856 as a runaway by John S. Hollingshead. Released 20 October 1856 to Mr. Hall.

Benett Chrismas: Committed 28 September 1856 as a runaway by John D. Clarke. Released 2 October 1856 to W. H. Faning.

Ellen Brown: Committed 28 September 1856 as a runaway by Robert Waters. Released 7 October 1856 to John E. Robey.

Anna & child: Committed 29 September 1856 for safekeeping by A. K. Hewitt. Released 7 October 1856 to John E. Robey.

Diana: Committed 29 September 1856 for safekeeping by J. W. Waring. Released 6 October 1856 to J. W. Waring.

John Harkness: Committed 28 September 1856 as a runaway by Robert Mills. Released 3 October to J. G. Mitchel.

Moses Bosman: Committed 2 October 1856 as a runaway by Robert Waters. Released 4 October 1856 to Washington Young.

Henry Jones: Committed 2 October 1856 as a runaway by L___ Hazell. Released 5 October 1856 to I. Mulligan.

Jacob Ross: Committed 4 October 1856 as a runaway by J. S. Hollingshed. Released 4 October 1856 as a free man.

Sarah: Committed 4 October 1856 for safekeeping by H. R. Maryman. Released 11 October 1856 to H. R. Maryman.

Champion Wesley: Committed 4 October 1856 as a runaway by: Released 6 October 1856 to N. McLain.

Harriet Humphreys: Committed 16 June 1856 as a runaway by James Ward. Released 10 December 1856 to R. W. Hunter.

Nace Hodge: Committed 7 October 1856 as a runaway by Francis B. Lord. Released 11 November 1856 to Charles Beall.

Romeo Mason: Committed 7 June 1856 as a runaway by James Ward. Released 10 October 1856 to Bladen Forrest.

Jerry Phillips: Committed 10 October 1856 as a runaway by Robert Mills. Released 30 October 1857 as a free man.

Albert: Committed 10 October 1856 as a runaway by James Ward. Released 20 June 1857 to District Sheriff.[6]

Charles: Committed 10 October 1856 as a runaway by James Ward. Released 20 June 1856 to District Sheriff.

Sylvester: Committed 10 October 1856 as a runaway by James Ward. Released 20 June 1856 to District Sheriff.

William: Committed 10 October 1856 as a runaway by James Ward. Released 20 June 1856 to District Sheriff.

Washington: Committed 10 October 1856 as a runaway by James Ward. Released 20 June 1856 to District Sheriff.

Laura & 2 children: Committed 10 October 1856 as a runaway by James Ward. Released 20 June 1856 to District Sheriff.

Bill Addison: Committed 12 October 1856 as a runaway by W. N. Fanning. Released 14 October 1856 to Mr. Mullikin.

Henry Barnes: Committed 12 October 1856 as a runaway

---

[6]In those cases in which release is made to the District Sheriff, the release is at the order of the U. S. Circuit Court. A search of records of fugitive slave cases may yield more information .

by James W. Baggott. Released 15 October 1856 to Mr. Bowie.

Ann & child: Committed 15 October 1856 for safekeeping by J. W. Kitchens. Released 5 November 1856 to John H. Smoot.

John Noyes: Committed 16 October 1856 as a runaway by J. W. Reynolds. Released 2 December 1856 to George C. Morgan.

Eliza Bowie: Committed 16 October 1856 as a runaway by J. W. Reynolds. Released 10 December 1856 as a free woman.

Cynthia Ann Dodson: Committed 20 October 1856 as a runaway by James McGowan. Released 24 October 1856 to James Spinks.

Harris Diggs: Committed 20 October 1856 for safekeeping by J. F. Wolland. Released 24 October 1856 to Gustavus Waters.

Betty: Committed 22 October 1856 as a runaway by James Ward. Released 24 October 11856 to John Hedgman.

Dorethy: Committed 23 October 1856 as a runaway by A. LaTruitte. Released 23 October 1856 to Mr. Kimbell.

William Thomas: Committed 25 October 1856 as a runaway by J. N. Gates. Released 2 November 1856 to Samuel H. Cox.

Thomas Spriggs: Committed 26 October 1856 as a runaway by Robert Mills. Released 7 November 1856 to Charles Clark.

Harry: Committed 27 October 1856 for safekeeping by Lewis Carusi. Released 11 November 1856 to Lewis Carusi.

Joseph: Committed 27 October 1856 for safekeeping by Lewis Carusi. Released 11 November 1856 to J. H. Stewart.

Henry Jones: Committed 27 October 1856 as a runaway by Joseph Williamson. Released 8 November 1856 to George Davidson.

Caroline: Committed 27 October 1856 for safekeeping by J. Murray Rush. Released 31 October 1856 to B. O. Sheckells.

John Duckett: Committed 30 October 1856 as a runaway by Thomas H. Robinson. Released 2 November 1856 to Smith Suitte.

John Williams: Committed 30 October 1856 as a runaway by Thomas H. Robinson. Released 5 November 1856 to Mr. Brooks.

Susan Holliday: Committed 1 November1856 as a runaway by J. G. May. Released 3 November 1856 as a free woman.

Charles Williams: Committed 1 November1856 as a runaway by J. G. May. Released 8 November 1856 as a free man.

Daniel Batson: Committed 7 November1856 as a runaway by W. H. Fanning. Released 8 November 1856 as free.

Frances: Committed 8 November 1856 for safekeeping by W. A. Boss. Released 12 November 1856 to S. H. Young.

Francis Stewart: Committed 14 November 1856 as a runaway by Ig___ Dean. Released 1 December 1856 to ___ Robey.

Francis: Committed 18 November 1856 as a runaway by James Donnalson. Released 1 December 1856 to James Spinks.

John Wood: Committed 19 November 1856 as a runaway by John H. Stewart. Released 3 December 1856 to ___ Robey.

Alfred: Committed 19 November 1856 for safekeeping by H. Magruder. Released 25 November 1856 to W. B. Beall.

William Culver: Committed 19 November 1856 as a runaway by Joseph Williamson. Released 4 December 1856 to Richard Jacobs.

Josiah: Committed 23 November 1856 as a runaway by James Ward. Released 10 January 1857 to E. Daniels.

Alfred Scott: Committed 23 November 1856 as a runaway. Released 1 December 1856 to B. M. Campbell.

Moses: Committed 24 November 1856 as a runaway by Joseph A. Gill. Released 2 December 1856 to S. A. Buckman.

James Hawkins: Committed 29 November 1856 as a runaway by W. H. Langley. Released 9 December 1856 to J. E. Yearly.

Nelly Johnson: Committed 29 November 1856 for safekeeping by J. W. Kitchens for Thomas Turner Jr. Released 11 December 1856 to J. W. Kitchens.

Louisa Johnson: Committed 29 November 1856 for safekeeping by J. W. Kitchens for Thomas Turner Jr. Released 6 December 1856 to James Spinks.

John Johnson: Committed 29 November 1856 for safekeeping by J. W. Kitchens for Thomas Turner Jr. Released 6 December 1856 to James Spinks.

Lewis Summerville: Committed 3 December 1856 as a runaway by Robert Waters. Released 5 February 1857 to J. C. Cook.

Sam Pleasants: Committed 4 December 1856 as a runaway by N. G. Sanderson. Released 3 January 1857 to W. J. Stone.

Nealey: Committed 4 December 1856 for safekeeping by General Briscoe. Released 15 December 1856 to General Briscoe.

Robert Johnson: Committed 4 December 1856 as a runaway by A. LaTruitte. Released 6 December 1856 to James Spinks.

John Addison: Committed 10 December 1856 as a runaway by N. G. Sanderson. Released 11 December 1856 to Norman Ross.

Martha Brooks: Committed 12 December 1856 as a runaway by Joseph Norwood. Released 12 December 1856 as a free woman.

Massom: Committed 19 December 1856 as a runaway by J. N. Gates. Released 14 January 1857 to B. O. Sheckells.

George Reed: Committed 26 December 1856 as a

runaway by J. W. Reynolds. Released 12 December 1856 as a free man.

Margaret Cooper: Committed 26 December 1856 as a runaway by R. Collins. Released 21 January 1857 to _____ Spencer.

David Grady: Committed 29 December 1856 for safekeeping by William Robinson. Released 5 January 1857 to William B. Robinson.

Phillip Brown: Committed 29 December 1856 as a runaway by James Sutton. Released 5 January 1857 to _____ Sheckells.

Louisa Brook: Committed 30 December 1856 as a runaway by J. W. Kitchens. Released 31 December 1856 to W. A. Wallace.

Thomas Dade: Committed 31 December 1856 as a runaway by Joseph Birch. Released 31 December 1856 as a free man.

Henry Johnson: Committed 31 December 1856 as a runaway by Robert Waters. Released 19 February 1857 to Daniel R. Dyer.

John W. Clark: Committed 2 Feb: for safekeeping by Thomas E. Kirkley. Discharged by order of the Circuit Court 29 March 1857.

Lewis Gassaway: Committed 15 October 1856 for safekeeping by ' Marshall' 29 March 1857.

Charity Gassaway: Committed 15 October 1856 for safekeeping by ' Marshall' 29 March 1857.

Rebecca Cooler: Committed 2 January 1857 as a runaway by J. W. Kitchens. Released 3 January 1857 as a free woman.

Daniel Bowman: Committed 8 January 1857 for safekeeping by Guy & Briggs. Released 16 January 1857 to John E. Robey.

Jarret Dyson: Committed 10 January 1857 for safekeeping by R. H. Trunnell for A. Dent. Released 24 January 1857 to W. C. Hazell.

Washington Proctor: Committed 11 January 1857 as a runaway by Cox and Kemble. Released 14 January 1857 to Thomas Marshall.

Rezin Gantt: Committed 11 January 1857 as a runaway by Cox and Kemble. Released 14 January 1857 to James M. Marshall.

Abraham: Committed 11 January 1857 as a runaway by James Ward. No release information entered.

Louisa: Committed 14 January 1857 as a runaway by Thomas H. Robinson. Released 2 February 1857 to David Barry.

Alfred Beams: Committed 14 January 1857 as a runaway by J. W. Gross. Released 5 February 1857 as free.

John Green: Committed 15 January 1857 as a runaway by R. J. Faullkner. Released 27 January 1857 to Mrs. Poole.

Richard Clements: Committed 15 January 1857 as a runaway by R. J. Faullkner. Released 27 January 1857 to Mrs. Poole.

Luke Helvins: Committed 15 January 1857 as a runaway

by R. J. Faullkner. Released
27 January 1857 to Mrs. Poole.

Noah: Committed 21 January 1857
for safekeeping by John
Hopkins. Released 24 January
1857 to W. Selence.

Rofus Simms: Committed
22 January 1857 for
safekeeping by George W.
Young. Released 21 February
1857 to William Sanderson.

Emma Triplett & child:
Committed 22 January 1857 as
a runaway by W. A. Bass.
Released 29 January 1857 to
Indiana Milstead.

Rachel Norton: Committed
24 January 1857 as a runaway
by A. LaTruitte. Released 26
January to Mrs. Cole.

Henry Johnson: Committed
27 January 1857 as a runaway
by John F. May. Release 9
March 1857 as a free man.

Barney: Committed 25 January
1857 as a runaway by Frank
Reilly. Released 28 January
1857 to Edward Ball.

Joe: Committed 3 February 1857
for safekeeping by J. H.
Phillips. Released 19 February
1857 to D. Naylor.

Jane: Committed 6 February 1857
for safekeeping by E. M.
Chafrin. Released 9 February
1857 to Joshua Gibson.

Basil: Committed 7 February 1857
for safekeeping by Jacob F.
King. Released 8 February
1857 to Jacob F. King.

Adam Brown: Committed
19 February 1857 as a runaway
by Joseph Gill. Released 7
March 1857 to Thomas Riley.

Thomas Duffy: Committed
19 February 1857 as a runaway

by R. H. Lusby. Released 9
March 1857 to J. E. Robey.

Mary Smith: Committed
21 February 1857 as a runaway
by William Cox. Released 7
March 1857 to J. R. Warring.

Louisa: Committed 23 February
1857 for safekeeping by A. E.
L. Keese. Released 25 February
1857 to A. E. L. Keese.

Andrew Jackson: Committed
23 February 1857 as a runaway
by Victor Bier. Released 6
March 1857 to Thomas L.
Bowie.

Thomas Davis: Committed
23 February 1857 as a runaway
by A. LaTruitte. Released 3
March 1857 to Shelby Clark.

James Williams: Committed
28 February 1857 as a runaway
by James Ward. Released 5
March 1857 to Dr. Peach.

Sandy Lynch: Committed
26 February 1857 as a runaway
by Robert Waters. Released 26
March 1857 to William W.
Allnutt.

Anthony Baltimore: Committed
27 February 1857 as a runaway
by N. Y. Sanderson. Released
28 February 1857 to Hy.
Stephenson.

John Allen: Committed
27 February 1857 as a runaway
by Richard Jenkins. Released 5
March 1857 to J. Duckett.

Alexander: Committed
27 February 1857 as a runaway
by George W. Duvall. Released
9 March 1857 to J. C. Robey.

Charles Ellis: Committed 2 March
1857 as a runaway by A.
LaTruitte. Released 9 March
1857 to H. McCeney.

Edgar Webb: Committed 2 March 1857 as a runaway by William Barnes. Released 11 March 1857 to Jonathom Magarity.

Hester: Committed 4 March 1857 for safekeeping by Francis Thompson. Released 11 March 1857 to Joseph Berrett.

Felix: Committed 7 March 1857 as a runaway by F. O. Callahan. Released 9 March 1857 to William Cox.

George Winters: Committed 7 March 1857 as a runaway by W. A. Boss. Released 10 March 1857 as a free man.

Edgar Webb: Committed 11 March 1857 for safekeeping by Jonathon Magarity. Released 16 March 1857 to Bruin.

Jim Hall: Committed 11 March 1857 as a runaway by W. L. Ross. Released 20 March 1857 to Mr. Blunt.

Cyanna Bowie & child: Committed 13 March 1857 for safekeeping by W. H. Birch. Released 17 March to Bowie.

Montel: Committed 15 March 1857 for safekeeping by James Forbes. Released 2 April to James A Madley.

Charles Crawford: Committed 20 March 1857 as a runaway by A. LaTruitte. Released 31 March 1857 to J. Maddox.

George: Committed 20 March 1857 as a runaway by A. LaTruitte. Released 25 March 1857 to Jerry Tonsend.

John Wesley: Committed 26 March 1857 for safekeeping by R. B. Hughes. Released 30 March 1857 to Phillip Mackey.

Boswell Dikes: Committed 26 March 1857 for safekeeping

by O. T. Vermillion. Released 4 May 1857 to J. C. Robey.

Jereldine Lewis: Committed 27 March 1857 as a runaway by Johnson Simonds. Released 28 March 1857 to Mr. Thompson.

Isaac: Committed 30 March 1857 as a runaway by Robert Mills. Released 1 April 1857 to Dr. Howard.

Lemuel: Committed 31 March 1857 for safekeeping by Rosanna D. Magruder. Released 7 April 1857 to Samuel Duvall.

Princes Garner: Committed 31 March 1857 for safekeeping by H. Maryman. Released 8 April 1857 to James J. Fowler.

William: Committed 1 April 1857 for safekeeping by B. F. Moxley. Released 13 April 1857 to Clement Hill.

John: Committed 1 April 1857 as a runaway by Richard A. Phillips. Released 5 April 1857 to Thomas Talbott.

Lewis: Committed 2 April 1857 as a runaway by Bailey Brown. Released 7 April 1857 to N. R. Richardson.

Nancy: Committed 2 April 1857 for safekeeping by Marshal. Released 17 June 1857 to David Fowble.

Robert Jackson: Committed 2 April 1857 as a runaway by Patrick McNickell. Released 22 May 1857 to Major Thomas Bauce.

Charles Levine: Committed 6 April 1857 as a runaway by E. McHenry. Released 25 April 1857 to J. H. Bradley Jr.

Lewis Levine: Committed 6 April 1857 as a runaway by

E. McHenry. Released 25 April 1857 to J. H. Bradley Jr.

Bill Fender: Committed 11 April 1857 as a runaway by J. S. Norwood.. Released 18 April 1857 to F. M. Boteter.

Joe Turner: Committed 12 April 1857 as a runaway by William Sanderson. Released 18 April 1857 as a free man.

Frank Contee: Committed 14 April 1857 as a runaway by Francis Ward. Released 16 April 1857 to Zack Brady.

Alfred Lee: Committed 15 April 1857 as a runaway by H. Atchinson. Released 17 April 1857 to J. R. Douglass.

John Jackson: Committed 15 April 1857 as a runaway by Hy. Atchinson. Released 17 April 1857 to J. R. Douglass.

Henry Thomas: Committed 15 April 1857 as a runaway by Hy. Atchinson. Released 17 April 1857 to Basil Baden.

Hinson Lee: Committed 15 April 1857 as a runaway by H. Atchinson. Released 17 April 1857 to J. R. Douglass.

George Lee: Committed 15 April 1857 as a runaway by H. Atchinson. Released 17 April 1857 to J. R. Douglass.

Catherine Marlowe & child: Committed 15 April 1857 as a runaway by James Ward. Released 11 May 1857 to Edward M. Clark.

Frances Scott: Committed 15 April 1857 as a runaway by James H. Suitt. Released 7 May 1857 as a free woman.

Harriet Brogden: Committed 22 April 1857 as a runaway by

James Ward. Released 23 April 1857 to Dr. Harden.

Jane: Committed 24 April 1857 for safekeeping by Michael Green. Released 4 May 1857 to J. e. Robey.

Eliza: Committed 25 April 1857 as a runaway by B. J. Watson. Released 1 May 1857 as a free woman.

Dick Shorter: Committed 25 April 1857 for safekeeping by A. H. Bean. Released 28 April 1857 to A. H. Bean.

Benjamin Lewis: Committed 27 April 1857 as a runaway by M. B. Farr. Released 29 April 1857 to Mrs. Dordett.

Dennis Gallaway: Committed 27 April 1857 as a runaway by C. Coffman. Released 12 May 1857 to Charles T. Woode.

John Perry: Committed 28 April 1857 as a runaway by J. H. wise. Released 29 April 1857 as a free man.

Frank: Committed 29 April 1857 as a runaway by A. LaTruitte. Released 6 May 1857 to James Somerville.

Henny: Committed 29 April 1857 for safekeeping by Benjamin E. Garrett. Released 8 May 1857 to J. C. Cook.

Henry Holland: Committed 2 May 1857 as a runaway by A. LaTruitte. Released 6 May 1857 to Samuel Wilson.

Isaac: Committed 4 April 1857 for safekeeping by N. Boyd Brooks. Released 7 May 1857 to N. Boyd Brooks.

Bill Armstrong: Committed 5 May 1857 as a runaway by Edward Swann. Released 16 May 1857 to J. C. Cook.

Robert Bowie: Committed 7 May 1857 as a runaway by Robert Rainey. Released 5 June 1857 to Dr. Turton.

Henrietta Holmes: Committed 7 May 1857 as a runaway by Robert Waters. Released 8 May to J. W. Ross.

Mary A. Holmes: Committed 7 May 1857 as a runaway by Robert Waters. Released 8 May to J. W. Ross.

Martha A. Holmes: Committed 7 May 1857 as a runaway by Robert Waters. Released 8 May to J. W. Ross.

George Sharp: Committed 8 May 1857 as a runaway William Horner. Released 14 May 1857 to Thomas H. Gairy.

James Sharp: Committed 8 May 1857 as a runaway William Horner. Released 14 May 1857 to Thomas H. Gairy.

Thomas Sharpe: Committed 8 May 1857 as a runaway William Horner. Released 14 May 1857 to Thomas H. Gairy.

Elizabeth Sharp: Committed 8 May 1857 as a runaway Wollard & Horner. Released 14 May 1857 to Thomas H. Gairy.

Sophia Sharp: Committed 8 May 1857 as a runaway William Horner. Released 14 May 1857 to Thomas H. Gairy.

Maria: Committed 19 May 1857 for safekeeping by B. J. Watson. Release notes not completed.[7]

Silva: Committed 25 May 1857 as a runaway by A. LaTruitte. Released 25 May 1857 to Dr. Waring.

William Spencer: Committed 26 May 1857 as a runaway by William Carries. Released 29 May 1857 to Edward Plater (Shorter?)

Christina Pinkney: Committed 26 May 1857 as a runaway by James Ward. Released 3 June 1857 to Mrs. E. L. Young.

Jefferson: Committed 31 May 1857 for safekeeping by W. Jones. Released 28 May 1857 to W. Jones.

Samuel Pratt: Committed 2 June 1857 as a runaway by E. B. Duvall. Released 10 June 1857 to Thomas H. Gary.

Frederick: Committed 3 June 1857 as a runaway by James Ward. Released 8 June 1857 to J. C. Gunnell.

Frank Green: Committed 4 June 1857 as a runaway by James Ward. Released 8 June 1857 to A. F. Boswell.

John Clifson: Committed 5 June 1857 as a runaway by Francis Ward. Released 9 June 1857 to Francis M. Butler.

Louisa Warren: Committed 5 June 1857 for safekeeping by N. Callan. Released 12 July 1857 to Dr. Morgan.

John Warren: Committed 5 June 1857 for safekeeping by N. Callan. Released 12 July 1857 to Dr. Morgan.

William Warren: Committed 5 June 1857 for safekeeping by N. Callan. Released 12 July 1857 to Dr. Morgan.

---

[7] Release notes refer to Criminal Docket June Term 1857, No. 32.

Sophia Lee: Committed 11 June 1857 for safekeeping by Joseph Williamson. Released 2 July 1857 to J. C. Cook.

Walter Wallace: Committed 12 June 1857 as a runaway by Linn & Waters. Released 19 June 1857 to Briscoe.

William Marble: Committed 15 June 1857 for safekeeping by A. E. L. Keese. Released 24 June 1857 to A. E. L. Keese.

Dilley Simms & child: Committed 16 June 1857 as a runaway by Robert Mills. Released 17 June 1857 to B. O. Sheckells.

Rezin: Committed 20 June 1857 as a runaway by Alfred Vermillion. Released 30 June 1857 to Lawson Vermillion.

South Carolina: Committed 30 June 1857 as a runaway by J. F. King. Released 3 July 1857 to B. O. Sheckell.

Frank Washington: Committed 2 July 1857 as a runaway by H. A. Atcherson. Released 3 July 1857 to B. M. Campbell.

Maria: Committed 2 July 1857 for safekeeping by B. Milburn. Released 10 July 1857 to Joseph Weaver.

Richard: Committed 2 July 1857 for safekeeping by William Hazell. Released 10 July 1857 to John L. Berry.

Maria Sewell: Committed 3 July 1857 as a runaway by Robert Mills. Released 8 July 1857 to J. E. Robey.

Phillip: Committed 4 July 1857 as a runaway by R. R. Burr. Released 9 Ju7ly 1857 to Dr. Lewis Mackall.

John: Committed 4 July 1857 as a runaway by A. LaTruitte.

Released 6 July 1857 to Brook Mackall.

Walter Dunnington: Committed 7 July 1857 as a runaway by A. LaTruitte. Released 21 July 1857 to David Young.

Dorsey: Committed 7 July 1857 as a runaway by W. L. Ross. Released 28 July 1857 to Catherine Maddox.

Peter Hall: Committed 8 July 1857 as a runaway by H. Yeatman. Released 31 July 1857 to C. Cook.

Sam Sims: Committed 9 July 1857 for safekeeping by J. W. Ketching. Released 26 August 1857 to James G. Essex.

Andrew Norris: Committed 10 July 1857 as a runaway by A. LaTruitte. Released 24 July to Henry Naylor.

John H. Butler: Committed 11 July 1857 for safekeeping by W. D. Bell. Released 13 July 1857 to W. D. Bell.

Thomas Diggs: Committed 13 July 1857 as a runaway by Robert Waters. Released 22 July 1857 to Hy. Dangerfield.

Harriet Churn & 2 children: Committed 15 July 1857 as a runaway by Reuben Collins. Released 28 July 1857 to Mary D. Loan.

Henry Rozier: Committed 16 July 1857 as a runaway by Frank Reilly. Released 17 July 1857 to Thomas Marshall.

John: Committed 18 July 1857 as a runaway by John H. Runner. Released 29 July 1857 to George Dent.

Nathaniel Crampton: Committed 28 July 1857 for safekeeping by

N. P. Causin. Released 3 August 1857 to W. C. Corre.

Caroline: Committed 29 July 1857 for safekeeping by John M. McCalla. Released 3 August 3 1857 to Margaret A. Miller.

Gabriel: Committed 29 July 1857 for safekeeping by Charles Sherman. Released 25 August 1857 to A. E. L. Keese.

Ann: Committed 1 August 1857 as a runaway by J. W. Gross. Released 4 August 1857 to J. W. Webb.

Granderson: Committed 2 August 1857 for safekeeping by James B. Pumphrey. Released 3 August 1857 to James B. Pumphrey.

Edward Simms: Committed 2 August 1857 for safekeeping by Richard Wallach. Released 21 September 1857 to William C. Corrie.

Alfred Solomon: Committed 6 August 1857 as a runaway by James Ward. Released 14 August 1857 to V. Taylor.

Mary Speake: Committed 10 August 1857 as a runaway by William Cox. Released 12 August to A. E. L. Keese.

Douglass: Committed 10 August 1857 as a runaway by James Ward. Released 18 August to Lewis D. Means.

Tom Jones: Committed 10 August 1857 as a runaway by W. H. Carries. Released 28 August to Richard F. Nelson.

Charles Johnson: Committed 11 August 1857 as a runaway by Charles Johnson. Released 2 April 1858 as a free man.

Maria Craig: Committed 14 August 1857 as a runaway

by William Hutchinson. Released 16 August to John Steed.

Charles Smallwood: Committed 13 August 1857 as a runaway by A. LaTruitte. Released 16 August 1857 to Horace Waters.

Harriet Henderson: Committed 17 August 1857 as a runaway by Robert Waters. Released 18 August 1857 to David Barry.

Fanny Ross: Committed 18 August 1857 as a runaway by A. LaTruitte. Released 4 September 1857 to Thomas C. Wheeler.

John: Committed 19 August 1857 for safekeeping by Basil Benson. Released 25 August 1857 to Hy Fairbank.

Joshua: Committed 19 August 1857 for safekeeping by Basil Benson. Released 25 August 1857 to Hy Fairbank.

Maria Savoy: Committed 22 August 1857 as a runaway by Owen Magee. Released 2 October 1857 to William Prater.

Aaron Draper: Committed 22 August 1857 as a runaway by James Ward. Released 3 September 1857 to Marchant Ricketts.

Henry Chase: Committed 24 August 1857 as a runaway by James Ward. Released 25 August 1857 to John Davis.

Jane Anderson: Committed 31 August 1857 as a runaway by James Jones. Released 2 September 1857 to Thomas Berry.

Mary & child: Committed 1 September 1857 for

safekeeping by F. Bell.
Released 3 September 1857 to
John E. Robey.

Anna & 2 children: Committed
1 September 1857 for
safekeeping by F. Bell.
Released 3 September 1857 to
John E. Robey.

Dick Anderson: Committed
2 September 1857 for
safekeeping by Edley Paul.
Released 3 September 1857 to
Edley Paul.

Andrew: Committed 5 September
1857 as a runaway by A.
LaTruitte. Released 7
September 1857 to J. W.
Cooke.

Tressa Tyler: Committed
8 September 1857 as a runaway
by W. Cox. Released
25 September 1857 to
Jane E. Beall.

Laurena: Committed
10 September 1857 for
safekeeping by H. R.
Merryman. Released
11 September 1857 to Phil
Mackey.

John Barney Johnson: Committed
14 September 1857 as a
runaway by W. Daw. Released
17 October 1857 to
Robert Patterson.

Joseph Diggs: Committed
14 September 1857 as a
runaway by Robert Mills.
Released 17 September 1857 to
John E. Robey.

John Blackstone: Committed
14 September 1857 for
safekeeping by A. Duvall.
Released 12 October 1857 to
Sam DeVaughn.

Henry W. Edelin: Committed
14 September 1857 as a

runaway by R. H. Diggs.
Released   17 September
1857 to George Morton.

Alfred Lyles: Committed
14 September 1857 as a
runaway by R. H. Diggs.
Released 17 September 1857 to
George Morton.

Nathaniel Brooks: Committed 14
September 1857 as a runaway
by R. H. Diggs. Released
17 September 1857 to
George Morton.

Leonard Craig: Committed
14 September 1857 as a
runaway by R. H. Diggs.
Released 17 September 1857 to
George Morton.

Matilda: Committed 15 September
1857 for safekeeping by Fox &
VanHook. Released 21
September 1857 to Fox &
VanHook.

Daniel: Committed 15 September
1857 for safekeeping by Fox &
VanHook. Released
21 September 1857 to Fox &
VanHook.

Virginia: Committed
15 September 1857 for
safekeeping by
Fox & VanHook. Released
21 September 1857 to
Fox & VanHook.

Ann: Committed 15 September
1857 for safekeeping by Fox &
VanHook. Released 21
September 1857 to
Fox & VanHook.

Lucinda: Committed
15 September 1857 for
safekeeping by Fox &
VanHook. Released 21
September 1857 to Fox &
VanHook.

Vina & child: Committed 15 September 1857 for safekeeping by Fox & VanHook. Released 21 September 1857 to Fox & VanHook.

Richard Simms: Committed 18 September1857 as a runaway by James Ward. Released 22 September 1857 to Washington Young.

Charles Perry: Committed 18 September1857 as a runaway by J. W. Clubb. Released 21 September 1857 to Sarah Warren.

John Stewart: Committed under *writ of attachment* 19 September 1857. Released 23 September to Isaac Scaggs.

Ann: Committed 21 September 1857 for safekeeping by J. W. Webb. Released 9 February 1858 to J. W. Webb.

John H. Butler : Committed 22 September 1857 for safekeeping by George Carroll. Released 31 October 1857 to Marshall.

Delia Smith: Committed 24 September 1857 as a runaway by James Ward. Released 24 September 1857 to F. C. Thompson.

George King: Committed 26 September 1857 as a runaway by J. U. Lloyd. Released 27 September 1857 to Mrs. Gadsby.

Maria: Committed 26 September 1857 for safekeeping by B. L. Watson. Released 28 September 1857 to W, W. Hall.

James Stewart: Committed 26 September 1857 as a runaway by J. F. Wollard.

Released 29 September 1857. Notation reads "Suit".

John Mahoney: Committed 29 September 1857 for safekeeping by Joseph U. Carrieo. Released 6 January 1858 to John R. Robey.

William Marshall: Committed 29 September 1857 for safekeeping by Joseph U. Carrieo. Released 29 October 1857 to John R. Robey.

Rachel Chase: Committed 30 September 1857 for safekeeping by John W. Gross. Released 29 September 1857 to J. W. Kitchens.

Aaron Welsh: Committed 30 September 1857 as a runaway by John W. Gross. Released 24 November 1857 to James Thicker.

Benjamin Butler: Committed 5 October 1857 as a runaway by Frances Reilly. Released 21 October 1857 to Townley Robey.

Charles: Committed 5 October 1857 as a runaway by A. LaTruitte. Released 12 October 1857 to Joseph H. Beadley Jr.

Louisa: Committed 8 October 1857 for safekeeping by John D. Bowling. Released 20 October 1857 to J. C. Cooke.

Milly Mattox: Committed 10 October 1857 as a runaway by Frances Reilly. Released 20 October 1857 to J. C. Cooke.

Mina Mattox: Committed 10 October 1857 as a runaway by Frances Reilly. Released 20 October 1857 to J. C. Cooke.

David Smith: Committed 13 October 1857 as a runaway

by J. H. Stewart. Released
20 October to J. C. Cooke.

Beverly: Committed 16 October
1857 for safekeeping by J. M.
Batt. Released 27 October 1857
to James F. Scott.

Matilda Smith: Committed
17 October 1857 as a runaway
by J. H. Suit. Released
29 October 1857.

Tom Thurston: Committed
19 October 1857 as a runaway
by J. F. Wollard. Released
20 October 1857 to
Fielder Magruder.

Henry Tratman: Committed
19 October 1857 as a runaway
by J. F. Wollard. Released
14 November 1857 to
F. M. Butler.

Eliza James: Committed
19 October 1857 as a runaway
by J. F. Wollard. Released 23
October 1857 to A. H. Settle.

John Wesley: Committed
23 October 1857 for
safekeeping by R. B. Hughes.
Released 30 October 1857 to
Phillip Mackey.

Sarah Boyd: Committed
26 October 1857 for
safekeeping by W. Marshall.
Released 29 October 1857 to J.
H. Wise.

Charity Ann: Committed
29 October 1857 as a runaway
by Robert Waters. Released
29 October 1857 to J. H. Wise.

Sarah: Committed 2 November
1857 as a runaway by H.
Yeatman. Released November
5 to Patrick Ryan.

James W. Frasier: Committed
9 November 1857 as a runaway
by J. a. Burden. Released

10 November 1857 to
S. Blanford.

William H. Mallery: Committed
10 November 1857 as a
runaway by M. B. Farr.
Released 12 November 1857 to
John H. Drury.

Andrew Gant: Committed
10 November 1857 as a
runaway by M. B. Farr.
Released 12 November 1857 to
John H. Drury.

Jefferson: Committed
12 November 1857 for
safekeeping by William Jones.
Released 18 November 1857 to
Mary Maro___.

James Perry: Committed
16 November 1857 for
safekeeping by J. W. Colley.
Released 25 November 1857 to
J. W. Colley.

Charles: Committed 18 November
1857 as a runaway by A. E. L.
Keese. Released 23 November
1857 to William Eversfield.

Emily: Committed 18 November
1857 as a runaway by A. E. L.
Keese. Released 23 November
1857 to William Eversfield.

Jerry Ogle: Committed
21 November 1857 for
safekeeping by J. W. Ketchens.
Released 28 November 1857 to
Dr. Railey.

Dallas: Committed 25 November
1857 as a runaway by Mack
Howland. Released 26
November 1857 to Isaac
Scaggs.

Levin: Committed 25 November
1857 as a runaway by C. F.
McCarthy. Released 26
November 1857 to Isaac
Scaggs.

William Campbell: Committed 29 November 1857 by Yeatman & Watson. Released 1 December 1857 to Charles Hill.

Francis Marion alias John Noyes: Committed 2 December 1857 for safekeeping by George C. Morgan.

Tobe Sanders: Committed 2 December 1857 as a runaway by James A McGowan. Released 3 December 1857 to Benjamin Cooley.

Sam Jackson: Committed 2 December 1857 as a runaway by N. G. Sanderson. Released 14 December 1857 to Basil Brown.

John Hall: Committed 3 December 1857 as a runaway by Francis Reilly. No release notes.

Peter: Committed 5 December 1857 for safekeeping by W. H. Birch. Released 8 December 1857 to W. H. Birch.

Maria Swain: Committed 6 December 1857 as a runaway by Thomas Donoghue. Released 6 December 1857 to Isaac Scaggs.

Stephen: Committed 12 December 1857 for safekeeping by G. U. Watkins. Released to J. C. Cooke.

Eliza Coursay: Committed 17 December 1857 as a runaway by J. F. Wollard. Released 23 December 1857 to H. B. Warring.

Sophia: Committed 20 December 1857 for safekeeping by Joshua Bateman. Released 24 December 1857 to John Davis.

Phillip Cooke: Committed 21 December 1857 for safekeeping by J. W. Kitchens. Released 22 December 1857 to J. w. Kitchens.

Charles Vigal: Committed 6 December 1857 as a runaway by J. H. Suit. Released 5 January 1858 to G. W. Keating

Josephus Marshall: Committed 9 January 1858 as a runaway by Ross & Suit. Released 27 February to James Mankins.

Sarah: Committed 25 January 1858 for safekeeping by J. H. Wise. Released 31 January 1858 to J. H. Wise.

John Cooper: Committed 25 January 1858 as a runaway by A. La Truitte. Released 2 February 1858 to M. Hamilton.

Isaac Jackson: Committed 27 January 1858 as a runaway by H. O. Higgins. Released 30 January 1858 to John E. Thompson.

Osborn Smith: Committed 6 February 1858 as a runaway by J. L. Wollard. Released 8 February 1858 to E. G. Ford.

Isaac Jackson: Committed 7 February 1858 for safekeeping by W. A. Waugh. Released 16 February 1858 to J. E. Thompson.

Charles Fairfax: Committed 10 February 1858 as a runaway by R. H. Waters. Released 12 February to Walters Griffith.

John Butler: Committed 10 February 1858 as a runaway by J. L. King. Released 19 February 1858 as a free man.

Tom Bond: Committed 16 February 1858 as a runaway by A. LaTruitte. Released

14 March 1858 to
Rector Pumphrey.

Mary Hammond: Committed
18 February 1858 as a runaway
by B. G. Watson. Released
26 February 1858 as a free
woman.

Anetta Carroll: Committed
18 February 1858 as a runaway
by J. M. Busher. Released
28 February to J. M. Busher.

Harrison Bingham: Committed
19 February 1858 as a runaway
by S, N. Chipley. Released
23 February to Mr. Smith.

Theresa: Committed 22 February
1858 as a runaway by J. N.
Gates. Released 25 February
1858 to Thomas B. Edelin.

Isaac Jackson: Committed
24 February 1858for
safekeeping by J. E. Thompson.
Released 20 March to
J. E. Thompson.

John Shephard: Committed
24 February 1858 for
safekeeping by Lloyd &
Shipley. Released 13 March
1858 to P. C. Riley.

John Lee: Committed 25 February
1858for safekeeping by
McHenry & Irvin. Released 9
June 1858 proven to be free.

Joseph: Committed 7 March 1858
as a runaway by B. T. Watson.
Released 16 March 1858 to
Thomas G. D. Bowie.

Mittery: Committed 9 March 1858
as a runaway by James Ennis.
Released 7 March 1858 as a
free woman.

John: Committed 10 March 1858
as a runaway by F. Reilly.
Released 16 March 1858 to
John Dean.

Sophy: Committed 13 March 1858
as a runaway by W. L. Ross.
Released 21 April 1858 to J. H.
Higins.

Elizabeth: Committed 13 March
1858 as a runaway by James M.
Minor. Released 16 March
1858 to Lewis Magruder.

Hester: Committed 15 March 1858
as a runaway by Robert Mills.
Released 20 March 1858 to
'Wood'.

David Curtis: Committed
19 March 1858 as a runaway by
J. W. Gross. Released 25 March
1858 to William H. Gunnell.

William Brown: Committed
24 March 1858 as a runaway by
J. W. Kitchen. Released 3 April
1858 as a free man.

John Wesley: Committed
24 March 1858for safekeeping
by J. F. King. Released
15 March 1858 to J. F. King.

Thomas Miller: Committed
24 March 1858 as a runaway by
J. M. Lloyd. Released 3 June
1858 to Charles M. Keys.

Emeline & child: Committed
25 March 1858 as a runaway by
Robert Waters. Released 25
March 1858 to J. C. Cook.

Washington: Committed 29 March
1858 for safekeeping by J. L.
Wollena. Released 1 April 1858
to S. P. Franklin.

Susan Hanne: Committed 4 April
1858 as a runaway by J. F.
King. Released 5 April 1858 to
W. B. Jackson.

Harriet Holmes: Committed
6 April 1858 for safekeeping by
R. B. Hughes. Released 14
April 1858 to J. H. Wise.

William Johnson: Committed
7 April 1858 as a runaway by J.

S. Waugh. Released 15 April to W. G. Robertson.

Henson Warren: Committed 11 April 1858 as a runaway by Thomas C. Dunn. Released 18 April 1858 to George W. Danson.

Ben Hines: Committed 12 April 1858 as a runaway by William Daw. Released 8 May 1858 to Thomas Davidson and Mich. Nicholson.

Janies: Committed 8 May 1858 for safekeeping by Yeatman. No release notes.

Charles Estep: Committed 11 May 1858 for safekeeping by John C. Estep. Released 17 May 1858.

Robert Henry Hughes: Committed 11 May 1858 as a runaway by Pat Wilson. Released 29 May to Charles Walten.

Henry West: Committed 17 May 1858 as a runaway by W. A. Malloy. Released 22 May 1858 to Stephen Belt.

Tom & Chloe: Committed 18 May 1858 as runaways by Robert Mills. Released 21 May 1858 by order of J. M. Wright.

Richard Brown: Committed 18 May 1858 for safekeeping by J. M. Wright. Released 21 May 1858 by order of J. M. Wright.

Phillip Contee: Committed 18 May 1858 for safekeeping by J. W. Busher. Released 24 May 1858 to Mitchell, overseer.

George: Committed 19 May 1858 as a runaway by Robert Thompson. Released 22 May 1858 to George W. Hillery.

Washington: Committed 20 May 1858 as a runaway by David Welsh. Released 22 May 1858 to Charles Contee.

Caroline Bowls: Committed 24 April 1858 as a runaway by T. C. Donn. Released 25 May 1858 to William Moore.

Henry & Bill: Committed 25 May 1858 for safekeeping by J. C. Robey. Released 25 May 1858.

Alfred: Committed 25 May 1858 for safekeeping by J. C. Robey. Released 25 May 1858.

Reuben: Committed 10 June 1858 as a runaway by T. I. Williams. Released 11 June 1858 to H. B. Darkey.

Charles Goddard Whiteman: Committed 8 June 1858 for safekeeping by R. McCartney. Released 9 June 1858.

Henry: Committed 5 June 1858 for safekeeping by William Campbell. Released 16 June 1858 to William Campbell.

Martha Perris & child: Committed 16 June 1858 as a runaway by N. G. Sanderson. Released 30 June 1858 by order of Charles Watter.

Archy Dyson: Committed 17 June 1858 as a runaway by T. C. Dunn. Released 9 July 1858 to J. H. Cook.

John Henson: Committed 22 June 1858 as a runaway by J. Gittings. Released 28 June 1858 to J. C. Cook.

Elizabeth Sims: Committed 17 June 1858 for safekeeping by G. W. Young. Released 29 June 1858 to G. W. Young.

Ann Young & child: Committed 24 June 1858 as a runaway by

H. C. Mitchell. Released
17 July 1858 to Owen Sheckels.
Charles Allen: Committed 25 June
1858 as a runaway by C. W.
Arnold. Released 28 June 1858
by order of John J. Scot.
Jane: Committed 26 June 1858 for
safekeeping by Robert White.
Released 30 June 1858 to
Spinks.
Susan Hill & child: Committed
29 June 1858 as a runaway by
F. J. Murphey. Released 30
June 1858 to Dr. William Jones.
____ Lindley: Committed 29 June
1858 as a runaway by F. J.
Murphey. Released 2 August to
Millen.
Isaac Scott: Committed 2 July
1858 as a runaway by W. H.
Fanning. Released 6 July 1858
to William H. Fanning.
Hannah: Committed 2 July 1858
for safekeeping by William H.
McVeigh. Released 3 July 1858
to James Spinks.
William Furgison: Committed
5 July 1858 as a runaway by C.
G. Eckoff. Released 21 July to
____ Harris.
Nace Blackson: Committed
11 July 1858 as a runaway by
Pat Wilson. Released 5 August
1858 to Dr. Mullikin.
Louisa: Committed 14 July 1858
as a runaway by H. C. Dorn.
Released 15 July 1858 to ____
Miller.
Bill Green: Committed 15 July
1858 as a runaway by N. G.
Sanderson. Released 21 July
1858 to Samuel Jones.
Romuel Mason: Committed
15 July 1858 as a runaway by
Charles Walter. Released 21
July 1858 to B. Forrest.

James Campbell: Committed
16 July 1858 as a runaway by
L. H. Chipley. Released 17 July
1858 to John Cook.
Charles Delany: Committed
22 July 1858 as a runaway by
James Ginnity. Released
23 July 1858 to Richard Butt.
Henny: Committed 16 July 1858
for safekeeping by G. W.
Phillips. Released by order
from Marshall.
Ann Maria Davis: Committed
15 July 1858 as a runaway by
Charles Walter. Released
31 July 1858 to John Bailey.
Martha: Committed 15 July 1858
for safekeeping by B. F.
Hodges. Released 26 July 1858
to J. C. Cook.
Maria: Committed 30 July 1858
for safekeeping by P. Clayton.
Released 3 August 1858 to
Adams Express.
Amanda Johnson: Committed
2 August 1858 as a runaway by
James Ward. Released 3 August
1858 to James Dickens under
orders from Col. Selden.
John Harkness: Committed
2 August 1858 as a runaway by
T. C. Doon. Released 9 August
1958 to ____ Mitchell.
Jim: Committed 2 August 1858 for
safekeeping by B. H. Erinsfield.
Released 25 August to J. G.
Robey.
Charles: Committed 4 August
1858 as a runaway by Charles
Walter. Released 7 August
1858 to Judge Dunlap.
Nathan Brooks: Committed
3 August 1858 for safekeeping
by John W. Gross. Released 14
September 1858 to Charles
Kenley.

Rose Gordan: Committed 4 August 1858 as a runaway by James Cull. Released 9 August 1858 to Carrol Brent.

Boy: Committed 13 August 1858 for safekeeping by I. A. Linton. Released 13 August 1858 to I. A. Linton.

Adeline: Committed 18 August 1858 for safekeeping by John C. Hamilton. Released 20 August 1858 to Joseph Bruen.

Harriet: Committed 18 August 1858 as a runaway by John I. Sean. Released 19 August 1858 to J. C. Cook.

Phila Nelson: Committed 18 August 1858 for safekeeping by J. H. Wise. Released 30 August 1858 to I. P. Chase.

Henry: Committed 20 August 1858 for safekeeping by John E. Robey. Released 25 August to John E. Robey.

Dick Ogle: Committed 22 August 1858 as a runaway by T. C. Donn. Released 26 August by order of William O. Talbot.

Luke: Committed 23 August 1858 as a runaway by T. C. Donn. Released 27 August to Drigges Brien.

Josias Tinker: Committed 28 August 1858 as a runaway by G. L. Gilberson. Released 8 September 1858 to ___ Robinson. [8]

Elizabeth Jones & Sally Woodward: Committed 29 August 1858 as runaways by S. W. Chipley. Released 31 August 1858 to Marshall Warren.

Tilghman Banks: Committed 24 August 1858 as a runaway by Francois Reilly. Released 30 August 1858 to Col. Hughes.

Ben Butler: Committed 30 August 1858 for safekeeping by J. E. Robey. Released 27 September 1858 to J. E. Robey.

Edward Washington: Committed 30 August 1858 for safekeeping by Dr. Crawford. Released 2 September 1858 to B. O. Sheckels.

Patisias: Committed 31 August 1858 for safekeeping by John Hoorer. Released 31 August 1858 to B. O. Sheckels.

James H. Sharps: Committed 6 September 1858 as a runaway by T. C. Donn. Released 9 September 1858 to William Hopkins.

Sandy Hanson: Committed 7 September 1858 as a runaway by G. L. Giberson. Released 7 September 1858 to H. C. Scott.

Harriet Williams: Committed 10 September 1858 as a runaway by James Cull. Released 11 September 1858 to Lewis Magruder.

George Dimes: Committed 9 August 1858 for safekeeping by W. H. Moore. Released 10 September 1858 to William H. Moore.

Philip: Committed 8 September 1858 for safekeeping by Henry Yeatman. Released 26 October 1858 to J. C. Cook.

Christina & child: Committed 16 September 1858 as a runaway by T. I. Williams. Released 20 September 1858 to W. H. Birch.

---

[8] Entry bears notation "Charles County".

Richard: Committed 16 September 1858 for safekeeping by J. W. Kitchen for Dennis B. Lyles. Released 27 September 1858 by order of J. E. Robey.

Eduard Allen (White): Committed 18 September 1858 for safekeeping by Jesse Small. Released 18 September 1858 to Jesse Small.

Townley: Committed 18 September 1858 as a runaway by James Ward. Released 20 September 1858 to S. A. Barbour, owner.

John Smith: Committed 20 September 1858 as a runaway by T. C. Donn. Released 27 September 1858 to J. E. Robey.

Lawrence Matthews: Committed 21 September 1858 as a runaway by I. L. Clark. Released 26 October 1858 to T. W. Thornton.

Luke Williams: Committed 22 September 1858 as a runaway by James Ward. Released 24 September 1858 to B. o. Sheckels.

Patience Prater: Committed 22 September 1858 as a runaway by Charles Walter. Released 18 November 1858 to _____ Blunt.

James Carr: Committed 4 October 1858 as a runaway by James Ward. Released 17 October to Dr. W. H. Bruce.

Robert & Charles Mason: Committed 8 October 1858 as fugitives by T. C. Donn. Released 11 October to James B. Franklin.

John: Committed 9 October 1858 for safekeeping by T. C. Donn.

Released 11 October 1858 to William H. Benson.

Rufus Jackson: Committed 9 October 1858 as a runaway by T. C. Donn. Released 11 October 1858 to William H. Benson.

George Diggs: Committed 10 October 1858 as a runaway by T. C. Donn. Released 12 October 1858 to Col. Suttle.

Henry Johnson: Committed 11 October 1858 as a runaway by James Cull. Released 28 October 1858 to George W. Wilson.

Boy Wesley: Committed 9 October 1858 for safekeeping by J. E. Robey. Released 9 November 1858 to J. E. Robey.

Boy Frank: Committed 18 October 1858 for safekeeping by Edlin. Released 24 October 1858 to Edlin.

Harriet & child: Committed 31 October 1858 for safekeeping by B. F. Gwynn. Released 13 December 1858 to J. E. Robey.

Marcelus Dyson: Committed 8 November 1858 for safekeeping by John Mankin. Released 9 November to John Mankin.

George & Andrew: Committed 9 November 1858 for safekeeping by H. Naylor. Released 17 November 1858 to H. Naylor.

Ten Negroes: Committed 9 November 1858 for safekeeping by Absalom Hall.

Released 19 November 1858 to
Absalom Hall.[9]

Matilda Miller: Committed
8 November 1858 for
safekeeping by H. C. Matthews.
Released 17 November 1858 to
H. C. Matthews.

Frank Chase: Committed
12 November1858 as a runaway
by T. C. Donn. Released
20 November 1858 to William
Turpin.

William Simmons: Committed
13 November1858 as a runaway
by Charles Walter. Released
16 November 1858 to
J. Hodgers.

Adam Woodward: Committed
13 November1858 as a runaway
by Charles Walter. Released
16 November 1858 to
J. Hodgers.

Bill Richardson: Committed as a
fugitive from Maryland 18
November 1858. Released to
Jesse Small, Marshall.

David: Committed
18 November1858 as a runaway
by T. C. Donn. Released
24 November 1858 to James G.
Gray.

Hester & Child: Committed
22 November1858 as a runaway
by T. C. Donn. Released 26
November 1858 to W. W. W.
Bowie.

Alexander Ringold: Committed
23 November1858 as a runaway
by James Cull. Released
22 December 1858 to
James Cull.

Henson Hawkins: Committed
24 November1858 as a runaway

by B. W. Furgison. Released 17
February 1859 to J. W. Kitchen.

Harriet Dodson: Committed
29 November1858 as a
runaway. Released 1 December
1858 to an unidentified aunt.

Caroline: Committed
30 November 1858 for
safekeeping by John L.
Deeffeifs. Released 1 December
to Henry Birch.

Thomas Hanson: Committed
4 December 1858 as a runaway
by Charles Walters. Released
5 December 1858 to Henry
Birch & Co.

Clara Taylor: Committed
6 December 1858 as a runaway
by John Mills. Released
21 December 1858 to Benjamin
Perry.

Joseph Ball: Committed
7 December 1858 as a runaway
by James Ward. Released
27 December 1858 to
James Ward.

Frank: Committed 8 December
1858 as a runaway by T. C.
Donn. Released 14 December
1858 to ____ McGruder.

John Steuart: Committed
8 December 1858 for
safekeeping by Richard T.
Wilson. Released to I. C. Cook.

Tom Gant: Committed
9 December 1858 as a runaway
by James Cull. Released
10 December to
Thomas F. Bowie.

Ossa: Committed 23 November
1858 for safekeeping by
J. E. Robey. Released 13
December to J. E. Robey.

Patience Jackson: Committed
11 December 1858 for
safekeeping by Thomas Osborn.

---

[9] This entry carries the notation
"public sale" in the released entry.

Released 11 December 1858 to J. C. Cook.

4 Negro Boys: Committed 12 December 1858 for safekeeping by Thomas Milburn. Released 13 December 1858 to Thomas Milburn.

Jack Howard: Committed 16 December 1858 for safekeeping by J. F. Wollard. Released 27 December 1858 to J. F. Wollard.

Bill Waters: Committed 16 December 1858 as a runaway by . Released 18 December 1858 to James Risin.

Emma Mills: Committed 17 December 1858 for safekeeping by Elizabeth Brown. Released 18 December 1858 to Elizabeth Brown.

Richard Diggs: Committed 22 December 1858 as a runaway by B. W. Furgison. Released 24 December 1858 to Clement Hill.

Frank Steuart: Committed 25 December 1858 as a runaway by J. Mills. Released 6 January 1859 to J. C. Cook.

Jack Rogers: Committed 26 December 1858 as a runaway by T. C. Donn. Released 3 January 1859 to J. C. Cook.

Peter Day: Committed 28 December 1858 as a runaway by F. I. Murphy. Released 3 January 1859.

Charles Harp: Committed 28 December 1858 for safekeeping by T. C. Donn. Released 20 January 1859 to William Forrest.

George H. Cain: Committed 4 January 1859 as a runaway by D. Rowland. Released 18 January 1859 to ' Mother'.

Edward Dorsey: Committed 6 January 1859 for safekeeping by Joseph Bersley for Richard Briscoe. Released 12 January 1859 to Joseph Bersley.

Five Negro Boys: Committed 7 January 1859 as runaways by James Cull. Released 10 January 1859 to Charles Jenkins.

Frank Jackson: Committed 7 January 1859 as runaways by T. C. Donn. Released 10 January 1859 to Charles Jenkins.

Six Negro Boys: Committed 12 January 1858 for safekeeping by Joseph L. Spaulding. Released 13 January 1859.

Rosetta Brown: Committed 13 January 1859 as a runaway by Samuel Drury. Released 20 January 1859 to William H. Birch.

William Jones: Committed 15 January 1859 as a runaway by T. C. Donn. Released 13 May 1859 to Col. William Selden.

Joseph Doras: Committed 28 January 1858 for safekeeping by Jed. Gittings. Released 3 February to J. Gittings.

John Curtis: Committed 29 January 1859 as a runaway by Charles Walter. Released 31 January to Charles Walter.

Milly: Committed 24 January 1858 for safekeeping by N. Callan.

Released 31 January 1859 to N. Callan.

Henrietta Queen: Committed 1 February 1858 for safekeeping by J. H.Wise. Released 2 February to Elias Frarins.

John _ Doras: Committed 31 January 1858 for safekeeping by Theodore Mosher. Released 3 February 1859 to J. Gittings.

Michael Muntz (white): Committed 5 February 1859 by Marshall for Contempt of Court. Released 10 February.

Mary Holland: Committed 10 February 1859 as a runaway by T. C. Donn. Released 11 February to L. & N. Suit.

Tom: Committed 12 February 1859 for safekeeping by G. W. Talbott. Released 14 February 1859 to G. W. Talbott.

Margaret Brown: Committed 15 February 1859 for safekeeping by J. M. Young. Released 16 February 1859 to J. M. Young.

Tom Bond: Committed 21 February 1859 as a runaway by Charles Walters. Released to R. Pumphrey 12 March 1859.

Joe Norris: Committed 26 February 1859 for safekeeping by John L. Defeif. Released 26 February to W. H. Birch.

W. C. Hare: Committed 26 February 1859 as a runaway by D. Rouland. Released 16 March 1859 as free.

Henry Queen: Committed 28 February 1859 as a runaway by T. C. Donn. Released 2 March 1859 to Birch Hook.

Charles Brown: Committed 4 March 1859 for safekeeping by W. Underwood. Released 5 March 1859.

Eliza Greenfield: Committed 3 March 1859 as a runaway by Charles Walter. Released 16 March 1859 to Birch Hook.

Joe Cook: Committed 17 March 1859 as a runaway by B. H. Furgison, Released 22 March to James G. Pumphrey.

William Jackson: Committed 19 March 1859 as a runaway by P. McKinnett. Released 25 March 1859 to B. G. Harrison & Edie Harding.

R. N. Smith (White): Committed 22 March 1859 for safekeeping by H. Reaves. Released 24 March 1859 as sailor at liberty.

James J. Landson: Committed 22 March 1859 for safekeeping by H. Reaves. Released 24 March 1859 as sailor at liberty.

Bill Watson: Committed 23 March 1859 as a runaway by T. C. Donn. Released 7 April 1859 to Manning.

Washington: Committed 25 March 1859 for safekeeping by Joseph D. Poole. Released 26 March 1859 to Birch & Cook.

Rose: Committed 29 March 1859 for safekeeping by B. Mackall. Released 12 April 1859 to B. Mackall.

Washington Brady: Committed as a runaway 11 April 1859 by Charles Walters. Released 25 April 1859 to Mrs. Anderson.

John Crump: Committed as a runaway 14 April 1859 by

Charles Walters. Released to Sydney Hodgson 12 May 1859.

Sophia: Committed 14 April 1859 for safekeeping by John Waters. Released 21 April 1859 to B. O. Sheckels.

Bill McBrown/ Mat Brown: Committed 16 April 1859 for safekeeping by William Jackson for C. H. Canter. Released 26 April 1859 to J. E. Robey.

Henry Bingham

Arthur Bingham: Committed as runaways 22 April 1859 by Charles Walters. Released 26 April 1859 to Col. Robert E. Lee.

Lucy Dover: Committed as a runaway 22 April 1859 by Charles Walters. Released 26 April 1859 to 'Master'.

Matthew: Committed 26 April 1859 for safekeeping by John A. Barber. Released 3 May 1859 to Henry Birch.

Emma Committed 27 April 1859 for safekeeping by William Darrell. Released 29 April 1859 to Master Darrell.

Thomas Nichols: Committed 29 April 1859 for safekeeping by William A. Bass. Released 4 June 1859 to William R. Woodward.

Nace Barnes: Committed as a runaway 22 April 1859 by James Cull. Released 3 May 1859 to James L. Boman.

Thomas Shorter: Committed as a runaway 7 May 1859 by Charles Walters. Released 16 May 1859 to William Warren.

Oscar: Committed as a runaway 7 May 1859 by Charles

Walters. Released 10 May 1859 to W. H. Birch.

Julia: Committed as a runaway 13 May 1859 by T. C. Donn. Released 13 May 1859 to Richard Harden.

Rose: Committed 18 May 1859 by G. Mattingley. Released 23 May 1859 to J. C. Cook.

Mark Brooks: Committed 23 May 1859 by John D. Clark. Released 25 May 1859 to 'Birch'.

Laura: Committed 18 May 1859 by Martha D. Duncanson. Released 27 May 1859. Sold by order of the court.

William Ryan: Committed as a runaway 28 May 1859 by H. Raven. Released 1 June 1859 to J. C. Cook.

Martha Johnson & child Ryan: Committed as a runaway 28 May 1859 by H. Raven. Released 1 June 1859 to J. C. Cook.

John Kittel: Committed as a runaway 4 June 1859 by Charles Walters. Released 7 June 1859 to Richard Williams.

Two men & 1 woman: Committed 9 June 1859 for safekeeping by Col. Robert Lee. Released 10 June 1859 to Richard Williams.

John H. Plummer: Committed as a runaway 9 June 1859 by T. C. Donn & William McLean. Released 22 June to John Bell.

George Seal: Committed as a runaway 12 June 1859 by John H. Johnson. Released 14 June 1859 to Dario A. Winston.

Negro Boy: Committed 15 June 1859 for safekeeping by J. W. Kitchen. Released 16 June 1859 to Peter Joneson.

Agnes Johnson & child: Committed 17 June 1859 for safekeeping by Marshall. Released 22 June to Daniel Witman.

Lethe Hatton: Committed 24 June 1859 for safekeeping by Mason Piggott. Released 28 June 1859 to Mason Piggott.

Mitty/Kitty King: Committed as a runaway 27 May 1859 by T. C. Donn. Released 27 June 1859 Samuel Crosley.

Negro Boy: Committed 27 June 1859 for safekeeping by Clark & Smith, attorneys. Released 28 June 1859 to J. C. Cook.

Negro woman: Committed as a runaway 28 June 1859 by Dr. Duvall. Released 29 June 1859 to Dr. Duvall.

Frank Barnes: Committed 26 June 1859 for safekeeping by E. Wroe, trustee. Released 30 June 1859 to E. Wroe.

G. Brown: Committed 27 June 1859 for safekeeping by Clark & Smith, attorneys. Released 28 June 1859 to John Davis.

Sally: Committed as a runaway by Charles Watters 16 July 1859. Released 18 July 1859 to Smith Suit.

Frank Chambers: Committed as a runaway by T. I. Williams 25 July 1859. Released 16 August 1859. No custodian cited.

James Smith: Committed as a runaway 25 July 1859 by T. C. Donn. Released 26 July 1859 to Butler.

Eliza: Committed 26 July 1859 by John G. Stafford. Released 27 July to John G. Stafford.

Four Negroes: Committed as runaways 29 July 1859 by L.

Downs. Released 2 August 1859 to Robert Kick.

Frank Committed for safekeeping 1 August 1859 by I. E. Robey. Released 6 August 1859 to I. E. Robey.

Daniel Marcellius: Committed as a runaway 25 July 1859 by T. C. Donn. Released 3 August 1859 to E. B. Addison.

Charles Watson: Committed as a runaway 25 July 1859 by T. C. Donn. Released 8 August 1859 to William Emmert.

Fred K. Wisher: Committed as a runaway 5 August 1859 by H. Reaver. Releases 11 September 1859. No custodian noted.

Charles Roden: Committed as a runaway 6 August 1859 by T. C. Donn. Released 8 August 1859 to T. C. Donn.

Charles Dulaney: Committed as a runaway 9 August 1859 by T. C. Donn. Released 20 August 1859 to T. C. Donn

Edward Lee: Committed 9 August 1859 for safekeeping by Peter Von Essen. Released 11 October 1859 to I. C. Cook.

Charles: Committed 11 August 1859 for safekeeping by I. E. Robey. Released 8 September 1859 to I. E. Robey.

Charles Henry: Committed as a runaway 9 August 1859 by W. A. Malloy. Released 9 August 1859 to W. A. Malloy.

Ann Ross: Committed as a runaway by L. Drury 13 August 1859. Released to Clarke Mills 13 August 1859.

Maria Brown: Committed 12 August 1859 for safekeeping by I. E. Robey. Released

15 August 1859 to William Shaw.

Daniel Clark: Committed as a runaway by 13 August 1859 by James Cull. Released 27 August 1859 to Thomas E. Berry.

Basil Patterson: Committed as a runaway by T. C. Donn 15 August 1859. Released 18 August 1859 to C. E. Eversfield.

Charles: Committed 15 August 1859 for safekeeping by I. E. Robey. Released 8 September 1859 to I. E. Robey.

Ann: Committed for safekeeping 18 August 1859 by P. H. Howe. Released 18 August 1859 to P. H. Howe.

Pompey: Committed for safekeeping 18 August 1859 by I. L.Hollingshead. Released 25 August 1859 to W. A. Roche.

Henry: Committed for safekeeping 24 August 1859 by I. E. Robey. Released 8 September 1859 to Turner.

Herbert: Committed for safekeeping 25 August 1859 by George Poe Jr. Released 15 September 1859 to George Poe Jr.

Edward M. Jackson: Committed as a runaway 25 August 1859 by James Cull. Released 30 August 1859 to ____ Duvall.

William Edmondson: Committed as a runaway 25 August 1859 by Charles Watters. Released 3 September 1859. No custodian noted.

John Henry: Committed as a runaway 31 August 1859 by I. S. Hollingshead. Released 2 September 1859 to J. C. Cook.

Reason Yates: Committed as a runaway 1 September 1859 by Charles Walters. Released 3 September 1859 to J. Hellen.

Missouri: Committed as a runaway by T. C. Donne 1 September 1859. Released 14 September 1859 to C. Stewart.

H. Cubbins: Committed as a runaway 1 September 1859 by Robert White. Released 8 September 1859.

John: Committed for safekeeping 6 September 1859 by J. E. Robey. Released 7 September 1859 to J. E. Robey.

Joseph Cook: Committed as a runaway 7 September 1859 by James Cull. Released 13 September 1859 to Benjamin Duvall.

Elizabeth: Committed as a runaway 7 September 1859 by James Cull. Released 13 September 1859 to J. E. Robey.

Harrison Higgins: Committed as a runaway 15 September 1859 by Charles Walters. Released 11 October 1859 to J. C. Cook.

Charles Dulaney: Committed for safekeeping 16 September 1859 by P. W. Dorsey. Released to P. W. Dorsey.

Richard Brown: Committed for safekeeping 17 September 1859 by J. E. Robey. Released 13 October 1859 to J. E. Robey.

Lloyd Cole: Committed as a runaway 28 September 1859 by Williams. Released upon payment of $ 45 by Hyatt.

James H. Kane: Committed as a runaway 6 October 1859 by B. H. King. Released 12 October 1859 to Price Birch & Co.

John Matthews: Committed as a runaway 12 October 1859 by B. H. King. No release notes.

Mary Jane Brooks: Committed for safekeeping by Elizabeth Hall 15 October 1859. Released 22 October 1859 to John Hall.

Jane Bell: Committed for safekeeping 17 October 1859 by Harriet Donohoo. Released 20 October 1859 to Harriet Donohoo.

Molly: Committed as a runaway 15 October 1859 by James Cull. Released 17 October to George Talbott.

Jack Dorsey: Committed as a runaway 18 October 1859 by Samuel Drury. Released 27 October 1859 to B. C. Sheckels by order from John Jones.

Jenny Bell: Committed for safekeeping 25 October 1859 by B. Mackall. Released 21 January 1860 to J. C. Cook.

Annie & child: Committed for safekeeping 2 November 1859 by A. B. Berry. Released 2 November 1859 to A. B. Berry.

Jim Henry Hawkins: Committed as a runaway 7 November 1859 by H. Reaves. Released 7 November to John Gibson.

Bob Bush: Committed as a runaway 10 November 1859 by T. C. Donn. Released 26 November 1859 to Jesse Kitchen.

William Cole: Committed as a runaway 10 November 1859 by William Cooper. Released 26 November 1859 by order of Marshall at the request of Hyatt.

Mary E. Dorsey: Committed as a runaway 18 November 1859 by T. C. Donn. Released 29 November 1859 to James S. Huten, Va. 29 November 1859.

Abby: Committed as a runaway 22 November 1859 by T. C. Donn. Released 21 January 1860 to Davis.

Thomas Gray: Committed as a runaway 1 December 1859 by T. C. Donn. Released 9 December 1859.

Charles Williams: Committed as a runaway 18 November 1859 by James Cull. Released 5 December 1859 to Osburn.

Emanuel Smith: Committed 6 December 1859. No release notes, no other committal notes.

Alfred: Committed for safekeeping 13 December 1859 by B. O. Sheckell. Released 14 December 1859 to W. R. Williams.

Mercer's Girl: Committed for safekeeping 12 December 1859 by T. L. Mercer. Released 13 December 1859 to Carroll.

Bill: Committed for safekeeping13 December 1859 by Benjamin Berry. Released 15 December 1859 to J. C. Cook.

Emanuel Smith: Committed for safekeeping13 December 1859 by B. P. Smith. Released 30 December 1859 to Dr. Smith.

Chris Bell: Committed as a runaway 14 December 1859 by James Cull. Released 11 January 1860 to G. Pumphrey.

Bill: Committed for safekeeping 22 December 1859 by R. H. King. Released 22 December 1859 to R. H. King.

Bill Dasher: Committed as a runaway 29 December 1859 by B. H. King. Released 9 January to G. W. Talbott.

William: Committed for safekeeping 21 December 1859 by Samuel Berry. Released 22 December 1859 to Samuel Berry.

Edward Bell: Committed for safekeeping 21 December 1859 by P. F. Berry. Released 10 January 1859 to P. F. Berry.

John Robinson: Committed as a runaway 30 December 1859 by William Cooper. Released 31 December 1859 to L. S. Bartholo.

Alice Evans: Committed as a runaway 4 January 1860 by T. C. Donn. No release notes entered.

Elizabeth Statley: Committed as a runaway 8 January 1860 by H. Reaven. Released 9 January 1860 to Mrs. Eaton.

Sam: Committed for safekeeping 10 January 1860 by J. W. Borroughs. Released 11 January 1860 to J. W. Borroughs.

Billy Gassaway: Committed for safekeeping 8 January 1860 by I. L. Suit. Released 4 February 1860 to I. L. Suit.

Harrison Lounds: Committed as a runaway 20 January 1860 by B. H. King. Released 27 January 1860 to Worthington.

Horace Brooks: Committed as a runaway 23 January 1860 by T. C. Donn. Released 1 February 1860 to L. L. Sommerville.

Edward: Committed for safekeeping 27 January 1860 by Thomas Berry. Released 28 January 1860 to Zack Berry.

Jacob Lyons: Committed as a runaway 28 January 1860 by J. H. Goddard. Released 29 January 1860 to Lewis Mackall.

Walter Lancaster: Committed as a runaway 5 February 1860 by P. McKenna. Released 6 February 1860 to John Neal.

Betsy Bowers: Committed as a runaway 22 February 1860 by James Cull. Released 1 March 1860 to George Duvall.

Lloyd Davis: Committed as a runaway 7 March 1860 by P. H. King. Released 9 March 1860 to E. Duvall.

Phillip Williams: Committed as a runaway 9 March 1860 by J. H. Johnson. Released 13 March 1860 to Mr. Smith.

Alfred Wheeler: Committed as a runaway 10 March 1860 by J. D. Clark. Released 13 March to Burgees/ Burgess.

Richard Wanton.: Committed as a runaway 20 March 1860 by James Ward. Released 21 march 1860 to James Ward.

George Chase: Committed as a runaway 21 March 1860 by James Cull. Released 26 March 1860 to McGregor.

Henry Dormas: Committed as a runaway 2 March 1860 by P. H. King. Released 1 April 1860 to Ellwood Shaw.

Ned Williams: Committed for safekeeping 22 March 1860 by Samuel Dixon. Released 18 May 1860 upon order from Dixon.

Mandred Harrison: Committed as a runaway 31 March 1860 by T. C. Donn. Released 4 April 1860 to Richard Peach or French.

Frederick Atkinson: Committed as a runaway 4 April 1860 by P. H. King. Released 6 April 1860 to H. C. Matthews.

A. Wheeler: Committed as a runaway 6 April 1860 by James Cull. Released 13 April 1860 to Thomas Grimes.

Harry: Committed for safekeeping 10 February 1860 by William H. Thomas. Released 7 April 1860 to I. L. Berrett.

Basil Chase: Committed for safekeeping 5 April 1860 by Allen & Keese. Released 12 April 1860 to Allen & Keese.

Joe Smith: Committed as a runaway 15 April 1860 by P. H. King. Released 15 April 1860 to B. I. Berry.

Strother Morton: Committed as a runaway 15 April 1860 by S. Drury. Released 16 April 1860 to Dr. Ashby.

John Gredy: Committed as a runaway 19 April 1860 by P. H. King. Released 24 April 1860. No other information entered.

Jim Contee: Committed for safekeeping 26 April 1860 by P. H. King. Released 26 April 1860 to James B. Wales.

Robert Brown: Committed as a runaway 26 April 1860 by P. H. King. Released 29 April 1860 to Dangerfield.

Maria Dorsey: Committed as a runaway 19 April 1860 by F. L. Murphy. Released 4 May 1860 to Reuben Collins.

John: Committed as a runaway 17 April 1860 by P. H. King. Released 26 April 1860 to J. E. Robey.

Charles: Committed as a runaway 17 April 1860 by Judge Dunlap. Released 28 April 1860 to J. E. Robey.

Isaac Cokeland: Committed as a runaway 6 May 1860 by J. H. Goddard. Released 12 May 1860 to J. D. Waters.

Ann Brent & child: Committed as a runaway 7 May 1860 by P. H. King. Released 16 May 1860 to P. H. Howe. Name 'Robey' 'appears in parenthesis indicating that Howe is probably an agent of J. E. Robey.

Daniel: Committed for safekeeping 9 May 1860 by P. H. King. Released 20 May 1860 to L. W. Brooke of Price and Cook.

Eliza Carter: Committed as a runaway 14 May 1860 by Robert White. Released 16 May 1860. No other data given.

Andrew: Committed as a runaway 14 May 1860 by P. H. King. Released 16 May by order of P. H. King.

Robert Harris: Committed as a runaway 14 May 1860 by James Cull. Released 15 May 1860 to W. D. Bowie.

Dennis Matthews: Committed as a runaway 15 May 1860 by James Cull. Released 27 May 1860 to Gassaway Winterson.

William Lee alias Jones: Committed as a runaway 15 May 1860 by A. B. S. Keese and Charles Walters. Released 12 June 1860 with notation "taken as a runaway, known to be free".

Mary Smith: Committed as a runaway 28 May 1860 by P. H. King. Released 13 June 1860 to Michael Duffy.

Moses Whitaker: Committed as a runaway 28 May 1860 by P. H.

King. Released 13 June 1860 to Michael Duffy.

Bill Beckett: Committed as a runaway 30 May 1860 by P. H. King. Released 2 June 1860 to William B. Bayne & R. B. Brashears.

Dora Simms: Committed as a runaway 10 June 1860 by B. W. Fergerson. Released 11 June 1860 to David Rollins.

John Medley: Committed as a runaway 30 May 1860 by P. W. McKenna. Released 10 June 1860 to J. D. Bodling/ (Bolden?)

John Plummer: Committed as a runaway 7 June 1860 by J. H. Goddard. Released 12 June 1860 to Francis M. Hall.

John McPherson: Committed for safekeeping 26 June 1860 by P. H. King. Released to J. W. Addison. No date given.

Henry Marlow: Committed for safekeeping 28 June 1860 by William Daws. Released 30 June 1860 to Price & Cook.

Charles Burgess: Committed as a runaway 29 June 1860 by James Cull. Released 30 June 1860 to William Gross.

John Downs: Committed as a runaway 2 July 1860 by John H. Johnson. Released 10 August 1860 to M. Duvall.

Ben: Committed for safekeeping 6 July 1860 by P. H. Fitzhugh. Released 10 September 1860.

Wesley Harris: Committed as a runaway 2 July 1860 by Samuel Drury. Released 20 July 1860 to J. W. Claggett.

George Cole: Committed as a runaway 2 July 1860 by Samuel Drury. Released 21 August by order of Samuel Drury.

George Johnson: Committed as a runaway 3 July 1860 by T. C. Donn. Released 10 July 1860 to Daniel Clarke.

Jacob Jones: Committed for safekeeping 9 July 1860 by P. H. King. Released 18 July 1860 to Mr. Bartholow.

Bernice: Committed for safekeeping 13 July 1860 by Richard H. Key. Released 16 July 1860 on order of Richard H. Key.

Sopha /Jopha Beall: Committed as a runaway 14 July 1860 by P. H. King. Released 3 August 1860 upon order of P. H. King.

Hannah & child: Committed as a runaway 14 July 1860 by P. H. King. Released 18 July 1860 upon order of P. H. King to William Gordan.

George Williams: Committed as a runaway 18 July 1860 by P. H. King. Released 20 July 1860 upon order of P. H. King.

Lewis: Committed for safekeeping 25 July 1860 by David Gordan. Released 26 July 1860 to B. O. Shekels.

Allen Mann: Committed as a runaway 1 August 1860 by T. C. Donn. Released 10 August 1860 to Allen & Kimble.

Washington Sims: Committed as a runaway 11 August 1860 by P. H. King. Released 15 August 1860 to Price & Cook.

Lewis Hodges: Committed as a runaway 12 August 1860 by Michael Duffy. Released 16 August 1860 to J. B. Carson.

Sandy Young: Committed as a runaway 13 August 1860 by P.

H. King. Released 22 August To Brooke Young and L. B. Scaggs.

James Scott: Committed as a runaway 16 August 1860 by James Cull. Released 18 August to B. Campfort.

Henry Butler: Committed for safekeeping 22 August 1860 by R. P. Jackson. Released 22 August 1860 to R. P. Jackson.

Emily Claggett: Committed as a runaway 3 August 1860 by P. H. King. Released 25 August 1860 to J. E. Robey.

Patrick Henry: Committed as a runaway 23 August 1860 by T. C. Donn. Released 2 September 1860 to B. G. Stonestreet.

Wellington Meridith: Committed as a runaway 23 August 1860 by T. C. Donn. Released 4 September 1860 to Edwin Nelson.

Washington Watts: Committed for safekeeping 31 August 1860 by J. Kitchen. Released 4 September 1860 to J. Kitchen.

Mary Henderson: Committed as a runaway 1 September 1860 by J. W. Barnacels. Released 13 September 1860 to B. L. Watson.

John F. Hawkins: Committed as a runaway 1 September 1860 by James Cull. Released 8 September 1860 upon order of James Cull.

Sandy: Committed for safekeeping 8 September 1860 by J. E. Robey. Released 26 September upon order of J. E. Robey.

Sarah Bell: Committed as a runaway 10 September 1860 by T. C. Donn. Released 10

September 1860 to J. F. Donaldson.

Charles: Committed for safekeeping 10 September 1860 by Dr. Jones. Released 29 September 1860 to John Davis.

Jacob Smallwood: Committed as a runaway 11 September 1860 by W. A. Maloy. Released 11 September 1860 to W. I. Berry.

George Bowl___: Committed upon attachment by the Marshall 15 September 1860. Released by order of the Marshall 16 October 1860.

Eliza: Committed for safekeeping 15 September 1860 by A. L. Yerby. Released 22 September 1860 to A. L. Yerby.

John & wife: Committed for safekeeping 15 September 1860 by J. E. Robey. Released 26 September 1860 to J. E. Robey.

Charles: Committed for safekeeping 29 September 1860 by George Keating. Released 7 October 1860 to George Keating.

John Curtis: Committed as a runaway 2 October 1860 by William Cooper. Released 6 October 1860 to G. H. Waters.

Betsy: Committed as a runaway 3 October 1860 by P. H. King. Released 2 November to W. T. Meridith.

Daniel: Committed for safekeeping 4 October 1860 by John W. Bowie. Released 5 October 1860 to John W. Bowie.

John Childers: White man sentenced to Richmond Penitentiary for 18 years. Committed by Officer B. L. Jones for safekeeping. Released 8 October to B. L. Jones.

Robert: Committed for safekeeping 10 October 1860 by John Little. Released 28 March 1861 with notation "sold to Cook".

Rebecca: Committed for safekeeping 13 October 1860 by Owen Carroll. Released 21 November 1860 to Owen Carroll.

Joe Cook: Committed as a runaway 13 October 1860 by F. I. Murphy. Released 29 October to John Duvall.

Robert Woods: Committed as a runaway 15 October 1860 by P. H. King. Released 25 October 1860 to J. T. Adams.

Lydia Haney: Committed as a runaway 16 October 1860 by T. C. Donn. Released 12 June 1861 to her mother as a free person.

Lot Rideout: Committed upon attachment by the Marshall 19 October 1860. Released by order of the coroner 29 October 1860. A. J. Joice being billed for fees.

Jasper: Committed for safekeeping 20 October 1860 by Thomas N. Wilson. Released 23 October 1860 to Richard Wilson.

John Mann: Committed as a runaway 24 October 1860 by W. Albert King. Released 12 November 1860 when proven to be a free man.

Robert Gross: Committed for safekeeping 26 October 1860 by Samuel C. Crawford. Released 27 October 1860 to L. C. Crawford.

Henry Barbour: Committed on writ of Fi. Fa. by the Marshall 10 October 1860. Released 11 October 1860 to E. H. Moore with bill being charged to Jesse B. Wilson.

Parker Redab: Committed for safekeeping 28 October 1860 by E. Bird for William Cooper. Released 15 November to E. Bird.

Thomas Jackson: Committed as a runaway 31 October 1860 by B. H. Fergerson. Released 1 November 18609 to J. C. Reeves.

Hazel H. Harris: Committed as a runaway 9 November 1860 by J. H. Goddard. Released 17 November 1860 to J. H. C. Coffin.

James F. Pettit: Committed as a runaway 9 November 1860 by J. H. Goddard. Released 17 November 1860 to J. H. C. Coffin.

Louisa Bryant: Committed as a runaway 10 November 1860 by P. H. King. Released 28 November 1860 to Price & Cook.

Ann Ross: Committed for safekeeping 16 November 1860 by William Daws for Mrs. Howell. Released 22 November 1860 to Susan G. Howell.

Alice: Committed for safekeeping 19 November 1860 by Thomas Milburn. Released 5 December 1860 to Thomas Milburn.

Samuel: Committed as a runaway 20 November 1860 by P. H. King. Released 20 November 1860 to J. C. Cook.

Margaret Langford: Committed as a runaway 22 November 1860 by J. H. Goddard. Released 23 November 1860 to Arthur Cooper.

Charles Watts: Committed as a runaway 30 November 1860 by P. H. King. Released 12 December 1860 to James Owens.

Grandison Marshall: Committed as a runaway 22 December 1860 by P. W. McKenna. Released 7 January 1861 to N. Stoneshut.

Elizabeth Smith: Committed as a runaway 26 December 1860 by James Cull. Released 5 February 1861 to J. C. Cook.

Frank Hawkins: Committed as a runaway 26 December 1860 by James Cull. Released 1 January 1861 to J. H. Turner.

John Henry Waters: Committed as a runaway 27 December 1860 by . Released as a free man 14 January 1861.

Delly and child: Committed for safekeeping 1 January 1861 by R. N. Darnell. Released 5 January 1861 to R. N. Darnell.

Bill Brooks: Committed as a runaway 2 January 1861 by P. H. King. Released 17 January 1861 to P. H. King.

Sandy: Committed for safekeeping 3 January 1861 by H. W. Claggett. Released 4 January 1861 to H. W. Claggett.

Joe Harrison: Committed as a runaway 8 January 1861 by P. H. King. Released 26 January 1861 to Dr. T. Jenkins.

John Cook alias Hawkens: Committed as a runaway 7 January 1861 by James Cull. Released 14 January 1861 to John Duvall.

Robert Naylor: Committed as a runaway 12 January 1861 by Keese & Busher. Released 29 January to A. D. Hamilton.

George Naylor: Committed as a runaway 12 January 1861 by Keese & Busher. Released 29 January to A. D. Hamilton.

Felis White: Committed as a runaway 17 January 1861 by James Cull. Released 19 January 1861 to Z. Bell.

Henry Johnson alias Frank Warren: Committed as a runaway 18 January 1861 by P. H. King. Released 1 February by order of Mary Clayton to William Lyons.

Isaac Snowden: Committed as a runaway 21 January 1861 by P. H. King. Released 30 January 1861. No other notes entered.

William Carroll: Committed as a runaway 8 January 1861 by P. H. King. Released 30 January to A. D. Hamilton.

George T. Anthony: Committed as a runaway 4 February 1861 by P. H. King. Released 26 March 1861 to Dr. Hardy.

Noah Scott: Committed as a runaway 7 February 1861 by P. H. King. Released 21 March 1861 to Dr. T. D. Hurtt.

Henry Loggins: Committed as a runaway 13 February 1861 by Jacob Ash. Released 22 February 1861 to William Barker.

Aloysons Dixon: Committed as a runaway 13 February 1861 by J. N. Gates. Released 14 February 1861 to Thomas B. Edelin.

William Smith: Committed as a runaway 21 February 1861 by P. H. King. Released 28 February 1861 to H. H. Crawford.

Eliza Thompson: Committed as a runaway 26 February 1861 by P. H. King. Released 27 February under order of P. H. King. No receiving agent noted.

Dennis Brooks: Committed as a runaway 27 February 1861 by P. H. King. Released 27 March 1861 as result of order from O. Sprigg following a suit. No parties to suit noted.

Edward Brown: Committed as a runaway 25 February 1861 by J. D. Clark. Released 7 March 1861 to James H. Hall.

Daniel Richards alias Henry Harper: Committed as a runaway 1 March 1861 by T. C. Donn. Released 7 March 1861 to James H. Hall.

Bill Payne: Committed 1 March 1861 by T. C. Donn. No offense listed. Released 12 March 1861 to John H. Stone.

Jenett Corsey: Committed 4 March 1861 by O. E. R. Hazzard as a runaway. Released 6 March 1861 to J. E. Robey for Mr. Warren.

Daniel Harrison: Committed as a runaway 4 March 1861 by James Cull. Released 6 March 1861 by order of James Cull.

Henry: Committed for safekeeping 26 February by J. E. Robey. Released 11 March 1861 to J. E. Robey.

Caroline: Committed for safekeeping 5 March 1861 by A. M. L. Forrest. Released 7 March 1861 to B. O. Sheckels.

Robeys Boys: Committed for safekeeping 8 March 1861 by J. E. Robey. Released 11 March 1861 to J. E. Robey.

Tom: Committed 1 March 1861 as a runaway by T. C. Donn. Released 28 March 1861 to Judge Messick.

Alfred Franklin: Committed 10 March 1861 as a runaway by J. H. Goddard. Released 28 March 1861 to E. Jordan.

Levi Thomas: Committed 11 March 1861 as a runaway by T. C. Donn. Released 18 March 1861 upon order of T. C. Donn.

Clora A. Clagett: Committed as a runaway 11 March 1861 by P. H. King. Released 19 March 1861 to William Duvall.

Busher Washington: Committed as a runaway 12 March 1861 by J. G. Barmacls. Released 28 March 1861 to J. M. Harrison.

Henry Plummer: Committed as a runaway 13 March 1861 by P. H. King. Released 26 March 1861 to Edward Hall for Mr. Bell.

Samuel Butler: Committed as a runaway 13 March 1861 by P. H. King. Released 19 March 1861 to Mr. Massi. (Massy? / Massey?)

Lucinda and daughter: Committed for safekeeping 15 March 1861 by Mrs. Peyton. Released 16 March 1861 to Mrs. Peyton.

Emily Carpenter: Committed as a runaway 16 March 1861 by P. H. King. Released 26 March to Bryan.

John Jones: Committed as a runaway 17 March 1861 by P. H. King. Released 25 July 1861 to Mr. Hammond.

John Lee: Committed as a runaway 22 March 1861 by

William Thompson. Released 25 March 1861 to Harper.

William: Committed as a runaway 26 March 1861 by G. L. Giberson. Released 29 March 1861 to Mr. Ball.

Samuel Dyson: Committed as a runaway 27 March 1861 by James Cull. Released 27 March 1861 to L. Higdon.

George: Committed 28 March 1861 as a runaway by J. H. Goddard. Released 29 March 1861 to Samuel B. Anderson.

William Johnston: Committed as a runaway 29 March 1861 by James Cull. Released 4 April 1861 to A. Gwynn.

Hannibal Scott: Committed as a runaway 29 March 1861 by James Cull. Released 4 April 1861 to Townsand.

Jim Dogans: Committed as a runaway 30 March 1861 by F. J. Murphy. Released 11 April 1860 to Burgiss.

Dilli/Delli Mulliken: Committed as a runaway 31 March 1861 by P. H. King. Released 11 April 1861 to L. A. Lodger/Ledger.

William: Committed for safekeeping 1 April 1861 by H. Naylor. Released 6 April 1861 to H. Naylor.

Paul Henson: Committed as a runaway 1 April 1861 by W. A. Mulloy. Released 1 April 1861 to Phillip Hill of Maryland.

Oscar Lewis: Committed on writ of Fi. Fa. by the Marshall 3 April 1861. Released 27 April to W. H. Lamon and George Phillips.

Henry Plummer: Committed as a runaway 5 April 1861 by . Released 17 April 1861 to

Thomas A. Duckett or his agent.

George Green: Committed as a runaway 6 April 1861 by Fred A, Neitze. Released (date illegible) to the Provost Marshall.

Nancy Braydin: Committed as a runaway 6 April 1861 by J. W. Barnacle. Released 13 July 1861 to C. M. Price.

Richard Robert Peters: Committed as a runaway 6 April 1861 by P. H. King. Released 17 April to Daniel T. White.

Lucy Washington: Committed as a runaway 6 April 1861 by T. C. Donn. Released 24 April 1861 to Joseph H. Mattingly.

George Thompson: Committed as a runaway 8 April 1861 by D. Coats. Released 15 April 1861 to Mr. Duckett.

Bill Brown: Committed as a runaway 8 April 1861 by P. H. King. Released 15 April 1861 to Dr. Duvall.

Five Negroes: Committed for safekeeping 10 April 1861 by Tom Robinson. Released 10 April 1861 to Tom Robinson.

Charles Henry: Committed as a runaway 11 April 1861 by P. H. King. Released 19 April 1861 to an agent of Mrs. Fitzhugh.

Martha Taylor: Committed as a runaway 14 April 1861 by P. H. King. Released 19 April 1861 to W. G. Robinson.

Henry: Committed as a runaway 16 April 1861 by James Cull. Released 22 April 1861 to James Turner.

John Bolden: Committed as a runaway 16 April 1861 by J. H. Goddard. Released 25 April 1861 to an agent of Mrs. Catherine Garon.

Jim Smith: Committed as a runaway 19 April 1861 by T. C. Donn. Released to F. N. Butler.

Bob: Committed for safekeeping 1 April 1861 by J. M. Burch. Released 29 April 1861.

David Snowden: Committed as a runaway 28 April 1861 by P. McKenna. Released 30 April 1861 to Mr. Shaw.

Joseph: Committed as a runaway 25 April 1861 by James Cull. Released 27 April 1861 to A. Tolson.

Moses Lee: Committed as a runaway 29 April 1861 by C. Walters. Released 8 May 1861 to George Peters.

Henry Brooks: Committed as a runaway 1 May 1861 by P. McKenna. Released 9 May 1861 to W. O. Talbert.

Washington Thomas: Committed as a runaway 1 May 1861 by P. McKenna. Released 9 May 1861 to W. O. Talbert.

William Harper: Committed as a runaway 1 May 1861 by James Cull. Released 6 May 1861 to Allen Dorsey.

Hillery Brown: Committed as a runaway 5 May 1861 by J. H. Johnson. Released 7 May 1861 to R. Pumphrey.

George Dorling (Dorsey?): Committed as a runaway 5 May 1861 by J. H. Johnson. Released 7 May 1861 to R. Pumphrey.

Robert Coleman: Committed as a runaway 5 May 1861 by J. H. Johnson. Released 8 May 1861 to Charles Claggett.

Frederick Shorter: Committed as a runaway 1 May 1861 by T. C. Donn. Released 5 August 1861 to Brooks.

William: Committed as a runaway 1 May 1861 by James Cull. Released 9 February 1862 by order of the Maryland Legislature.

William Tell: Committed for safekeeping 2 May 1861 by William E. Hamilton. Released 29 May 1861 to William T. Hamilton.

William: Committed as a runaway 2 May 1861 by T. C. Donn. Released 13 May 1861 to Joseph Manning.

Dick: Committed as a runaway 5 May 1861 by James Cull. Released 22 May 1861 to Thomas W. Berry.

Isaac: Committed as a runaway 5 May 1861 by James Cull. Released 15 May 1861 to M. Coffree.

Charles Hall: Committed as a runaway 8 May 1861 by W. A. Mulloy. Released 11 May 1861 to M. Bell.

Samuel Carroll: Committed as a runaway 8 May 1861 by W. A. Mulloy. Released 11 May 1861 to M. Bell.

Anderson Hall: Committed as a runaway 8 May 1861 by W. A. Mulloy. Released 11 May 1861 to M. Bell.

George Pooley: Committed as a runaway 8 May 1861 by W. A. Mulloy. Released 11 May 1861 to J. H. Richardson.

Henry Isaacs: Committed as a runaway 8 May 1861 by W. A. Mulloy. Released 11 May 1861 to F. N. Butler.

Frank Butler: Committed as a runaway 8 May 1861 by W. A. Mulloy. Released 11 May 1861 to F. N. Butler.

Charles Carroll: Committed as a runaway 6 May 1861 by James Cull. Released 9 May 1861 to W. O. Talbert.

Henry Lee: Committed as a runaway 6 May 1861 by James Cull. Released 9 May 1861 to W. O. Talbert.

Dennis: Committed as a runaway 6 May 1861 by James Cull. Released 9 May 1861 to W. O. Talbert.

Thomas Riggin: Committed as a runaway 6 May 1861 by T. C. Donn. Released 7 May 1861 to Walter B. King.

Joe Thomas: Committed as a runaway 6 May 1861 by T. C. Donn. Released 11 May 1861 to B. Tolson.

Servant Gent: Committed as a runaway 6 May 1861 by John H. Waters. Released 10 June 1861 to John H. Waters.

Robert Butler: Committed as a runaway 7 May 1861 by James Cull. Noted as slave of L. Garner. Released 21 May 1861 to J. M. Gates.

Henry Smith: Committed as a runaway 8 May 1861 by T. C. Donn. Released 15 May 1861 to W. H. Curtis.

Edward Jones: Committed as a runaway 7 May 1861 by J. M. Johnson. Noted as a slave of Z. Berry. Released 18 May to Thomas Talbert.

Isaac Taylor: Committed as a runaway 9 May 1861 by T. C. Donn. Released 15 June 1861 to Resin Arnold.

Jim: Committed as a runaway 9 May 1861 by H. J. Murphy. Released 19 May 1861 to John W. Burke.

John Davis: Committed as a runaway 9 May 1861 by James Cull. Released 11 May 1861 to ___ Bell.

John Peterson: Committed as a runaway 10 May 1861 by W. A. Malloy. Released 27 May 1861 to John Smith.

John Alestock alias Welford: Committed as a runaway 10 May 1861 by W. A. King. Released 9 February 1862 by order of the Secretary of State.

George W. Smith: Committed as a runaway 12 May 1861 by William H. Robinson. Released 21 May 1861 to W. F. Harrison.

Frederick H. Bush: Committed as a runaway 12 May 1861 by James Cull. Released 21 May 1861 to Z. V. Posey.

Biller Simpson: Committed as a runaway 12 May 1861 by J. H. Goddard. Released 20 May 1861 to John Young.

Henry James: Committed as a runaway 12 May 1861 by J. H. Goddard. Released 20 May 1861 to William Young.

Stephen Frederick: Committed as a runaway 12 May 1861 by James Cull. Released 21 May 1861 to Z. V. Posey.

George Lee: Committed for safekeeping 12 May 1861 by

W. O. Talbert. Released 23 July 1861 to _ A. Osburn.

Abraham Taylor: Committed as a runaway 14 May 1861 by James Cull. Released 21 May 1861 to E. V. Posey.

James Hawkins: Committed as a runaway 14 May 1861 by James Cull. Released 27 May 1861 to George D. Hunt.

George Lyles: Committed as a runaway 14 May 1861 by James Cull. Released 17 May 1861 to J. L. Nally.

John Brown: Committed as a runaway 15 May 1861 by F. J. Murphy. Released 21 May 1861 to P. C. Pettit.

John W. Smith: Committed as a runaway 15 May 1861 by James Cull. Released 24 May to E. V. Posey.

George Reaves: Committed as a runaway 17 May 1861 by James Cull. Released 24 May 1861 to E. V. Posey.

Anthony Crawford: Committed as a runaway 17 May 1861 by James Cull. Released 18 May 1861 to J. Duckett.

William Hays: Committed as a runaway 18 May 1861 by James Cull. Released 23 May 1861 to George W. Duvall.

David Egelon: Committed as a runaway 18 May 1861 by James Cull. Released 23 May 1861 to George W. Duvall.

Abraham Nikols: Committed as a runaway 18 May 1861 by James Cull. Released 23 May 1861 to George W. Duvall.

Charles Stoddard: Committed as a runaway 18 May 1861 by James Cull. Released 23 May 1861 to George W. Duvall.

James Moken: Committed as a runaway 18 May 1861 by James Cull. Released 25 May 1861 to George W. Duvall.

Lewis Douglass: Committed as a runaway 18 May 1861 by T. C. Donn. Released 22 May 1861 to William D. Brooks.

Jack Butler: Committed as a runaway 20 May 1861 by T. C. Donn. Released 22 May 1861 to J. A. Osburn.

Henson Lee: Committed as a runaway 21 May 1861 by James Cull. Released 25 May 1861 to M. Gwynn.

John Baptist: Committed as a runaway 21 May 1861 by James Cull. Released 25 May 1861 to Thomas Williamson.

Matthew Mathias: Committed as a runaway 21 May 1861 by James Cull. Released 28 May 1861 to E. V. Posey.

William Besom: Committed as a runaway 21 May 1861 by James Cull. Released 28 May 1861 to E. V. Posey.

William Briscoe: Committed as a runaway 21 May 1861 by James Cull. Released 28 May 1861 to E. V. Posey.

Benjamin Brown: Committed as a runaway 21 May 1861 by James Cull. Released 28 May 1861 to E. V. Posey.

Andrew Bush: Committed as a runaway 21 May 1861 by T. C. Donn. Released 23 May 1861 to J. G. Pumphrey.

Henry Johnson: Committed as a runaway 21 May 1861 by James H. Suit. Released 26 May 1861 to William C. Pierce.

John Magruder: Committed as a runaway 21 May 1861 by B. D. Cloffer. Released 23 May 1861 to W. Bowie.

John Brooks: Committed as a runaway 21 May 1861 by Charles Walters. Released 22 May 1861.

Addison Brooks: Committed as a runaway 21 May 1861 by Charles Walters. Released 22 May 1861.

Alfred Matthews: Committed as a runaway 25 May 1861 by Patrick McKenna. Released 26 May 1861 to George W. Talbert.

Solomon Sprigg: Committed as a runaway 25 May 1861 by Charles Walters. Released 29 May 1861 to A. A. Ball.

Joe: Committed as a runaway 25 May 1861 by John H. Goddard. Released 25 May 1861 to E. H. Noble.

Henry White: Committed as a runaway 25 May 1861 by Solomon Goddard. Released 5 June 1861 as free.

Sally Johnson: Committed as a runaway 25 May 1861 by T. C. Donn. Released 15 June 1861 as free.

William _____: Committed as a runaway 26 May 1861 by James Cull. Released 15 June 1861 to Joseph H. Mattingly.

Joe Tyler: Committed as a runaway 6 June 1861 by Jacob Ash. Released to D. Lancaster. Date is illegible.

John Linus/Lewis: Committed as a runaway 1 June 1861 by Patrick McKenna. Released 18 September 1861 as free.

John Hawkins: Committed as a runaway 2 June 1861 by T. C. Donn. Released 21 June on writ of Habeas Corpus from Judge Merrick.

Henry Brown: Committed as a runaway 3 June 1861 by Charles Walters. Released 4 June 1861 to Franklin Reeves.

Abraham Taylor: Committed as a runaway June 1861 by James Cull. Released 20 June 1861 to E. V. Posey.

Alexander Realey: Committed as a runaway 5 June 1861 by J. W. Barnacle. Released 11 September 1861 to B. L. Watson.

Rederick Addison: Committed as a runaway 6 June 1861 by James Cull. Released 14 June 1861 to J. Bowie.

_____ Addison: Committed as a runaway 6 June 1861 by James Cull. Released 14 June 1861 to J. Bowie.

Ellen ___: Committed as a runaway 6 June 1861 by Charles Walters. Released 7 June to James Anderson.

Jacob Davis: Committed as a runaway 6 June 1861 by Patrick McKenna. Released 178 June 1861 to John Smith.

Dennis: Committed for safekeeping 10 June 1861 by William A. Webb. Released 11 June 1861 to William A. Webb.

Joshua: Committed for safekeeping 10 June 1861 by William A. Webb. Released 11 June 1861 to William A. Webb.

Thomas Rigdon: Committed as a runaway 15 June 1861 by

J. D. Clarke. Released 15 June 1861 to Walter B. King.

Robert Lanahorn: Committed as a runaway 13 June 1861 by James Cull. Released 25 June 1861 to Henry J. Barr.

James Wallace: Committed as a runaway 13 June 1861 by J. W. Barnacle. Released 15 June 1861 to T. W. Eversfield.

Mat: Committed for safekeeping 13 June 1861 by Thomas Claggett. Released 15 June 1861 to Thomas Claggett.

Robert Brown: Committed as a runaway 14 June 1861 by T. C. Donn. Released 18 June 1861 to H. H. Crawford.

Hortence: Committed for safekeeping 15 June 1861 by John Little. Released 25 June 1861 to John Little.

Nace Hawkins: Committed as a runaway 16 June 1861 by W. Thompson. Released to Edward Suit.

William Colbert: Committed as a runaway 16 June 1861 by J. H Johnson. Released 18 June 1861 to W. H. Wells.

Maria Goldsmith: Committed as a runaway 16 June 1861 by J. H Johnson. Released 20 June 1861.

Jesse H. Harris: Committed as a runaway 16 June 1861 by . Released 19 June 1861 to F. W. Butler.

Thomas Bruce: Committed as a runaway 16 June 1861 by . Released 19 June 1861 to F. W. Butler.

William Smith: Committed as a runaway 18 June 1861 by P.

McKenna. Released 25 June 1861 to H. H. Crawford.

William Brown: Committed as a runaway 18 June 1861 by P. McKenna. Released 25 June 1861 to H. H. Crawford.

Jim Lee: Committed as a runaway 18 June 1861 by W. A. King. Released 20 June 1861 to J. F. _____.

Ambrose Sills: Committed as a runaway 18 June 1861 by George W. Duvall. Released 25 June 1861 to E. V. Posey.

Samuel Jackson: Committed as a runaway 20 June 1861 by George W. Duvall. Released 3 August 1861 to J. W. Talbert.

Isiah Speaks: Committed as a runaway 20 June 1861 by T. C. Donn. Released 28 June 1861 to George Diggs.

John Moore: Committed as a runaway 20 June 1861 by G. L. Giberson. Released 15 July 1861 as free.

George Taylor: Committed as a runaway 23 June 1861 by James Cull. Released 28 June 1861 to James Diggs.

Henry Banks alias Monroe: Committed as a runaway 23 June 1861 by P. McKenna. Released 9 December 1861 by order of A. Porter to the Provost Marshall.

Thomas Bruce: Committed as a runaway 25 June 1861 by J. W. Barnacle. Released 28 June 1861 to Davin Brady.

Robert Adams: Committed as a runaway 25 June 1861 by J. W. Barnacle. Released 10 July 1861 to J. W. Bell.

John Thomas: Committed as a runaway 25 June 1861 by T.

C. Donn. Released 6 July 1861 to George Gaither.

John H. Brown: Committed as a runaway 1 July 1861 by T. C. Donn. Released 4 July 1861 to John Smith.

Charles Sullivan: Committed as a runaway 1 July 1861 by T. C. Donn. Released 29 July 1861.

James Posey: Committed as a runaway 1 July 1861 by James Cull. Released 26 July 1861 to George W. Duvall.

Henry Smallwood: Committed as a runaway 1 July 1861 by James Cull. Released 26 July 1861 to William Berry.

John Watson: Committed as a runaway 1 July 1861 by James Cull. Released 26 July 1861 to William Berry.

William Brown: Committed as a runaway 2 July 1861 by James Cull. Released 4 July 1861 to J. P. Pumphrey.

Conner Griffin: Committed as a runaway 1 July 1861 by T. C. Donn. Released 5 July 1861 to Thomas Williams.

Howard Griffin: Committed as a runaway 1 July 1861 by T. C. Donn. Released 5 July 1861 to Thomas Williams.

_____ Smallwood: Committed as a runaway 1 July 1861 by James Cull. Released 26 July 1861 to Thomas Mason.

Richard Diggs: Committed as a runaway 2 July 1861 by James Cull. Released to F. N. Boteler.

William Till: Committed as a runaway 1 July 1861 by T. C. Donn. Released to William B. T. Neal 14 July 1861.

Charles Rogers: Committed as a runaway 3 July 1861 by T. C. Donn. Released to R. King 1 August 1861.

Corneluis: Committed as a runaway 5 July 1861 by T. C. Donn and George Duvall. Released to James H. Johnson 19 July 1861.

Ben Matener: Committed as a runaway 6 July 1861 by W. A. Malloy. Released 6 July 1861 to Mr. Boland.

John H. Butler: Committed as a runaway 6 July 1861 by W. A. Malloy. Released 9 July 1861 to John Smith.

Henry Bowie: Committed as a runaway 7 July 1861 by James Cull. Released to Thomas Davidson 17 July 1861.

Moses Ogle: Committed as a runaway 7 July 1861 by James Cull. Released to Thomas Davidson 17 July 1861.

John Mitchell: Committed as a runaway 7 July 1861 by William Thompson. Released 15 July 1861 to Dr. Cook.

Charles Gordon: Committed for safekeeping 8 July 1861 by George Parker. Released 19 November 1861 to George Parker.

Jacob Cole: Committed for safekeeping 8 July 1861 by Charles Lyons. Released 7 August 1861 to Charles Lyons.

Dallas Etchinson: Committed as a runaway 7 July 1861 by Mrs. Albert King. Released 9 September 1861.

Annie Carroll: Committed as a runaway 7 July 1861 by P. H. King. Released 24 July 18651 to Thomas E. Berry.

James Freeman: Committed as a runaway 12 July 1861 by T. C. Donn. Released to John Smith 12 July 1861.

James Franklin: Committed as a runaway 14 July 1861 by James Cull. Released to G. Magruder 17 July 1861.

Adam Smith: Committed as a runaway 14 July 1861 by James Cull. Released to G. W. Duvall 17 July 1861.

Henry James: Committed as a runaway 14 July 1861 by James Cull. Released to G. W. Duvall 17 July 1861.

James Monroe: Committed as a runaway 14 July 1861 by Patrick McKenna. Released 9 December 18651 to the Provost Marshall (A. Porter).

Henry Monroe: Committed as a runaway 14 July 1861 by Patrick McKenna. Released 9 December 18651 to the Provost Marshall (A. Porter).

Agnes: Committed for safekeeping 15 July 1861 by George H. Barnell. Released 1 October 1861 to George H. Barnell.

Solomon Foot: Committed as a runaway 14 July 1861 by James Cull. Released to W. B. Cross 27 July 1861.

Joseph Speaks: Committed as a runaway 12 July 1861 by T. C. Donn. Released to A. Porter, Provost Marshall 9 December 1861.

Wesley Snowden: Committed as a runaway 16 July 1861 by

Allen Dodge. Released ___ August 1861 to Allen Dodge.

George Smith: Committed as a runaway 16 July 1861 by John D. Clarke. Released 19 July 1861.

Charles Farmer: Committed as a runaway 16 July 1861 by James Cull. Released 30 August 1861 to C. L. Gardiner.

George Singleton: Committed as a runaway 20 July 1861 by John H. Johnson. Released to C___ Alexander.

Benjamin Carter: Committed as a runaway 22 July 1861 by James Cull. Released 10 September 1861 to William Manning.

Adam Wordman: Committed as a runaway 22 July 1861 by James Cull. Released to Richard O. Hodges.

Griffin Carter: Committed as a runaway 22 July 1861 by James Cull. Released 10 September 1861 to William Manning.

____ Short: Committed as a runaway 22 July 1861 by James Cull. Released 8 August 1861 to Evan Adams.

Charles Jackson: Committed as a runaway 21 July 1861 by Henry Rivers. Released 9 December 1861 to A. Porter, Provost Marshall.

William Ford: Committed as a runaway 19 July 1861 by T. C. Donn. Released 22 July 1861 to A. B. Davis.

Walter Ford: Committed as a runaway 19 July 1861 by T. C. Donn. Released 22 July 1861 to A. B. Davis.

Albert Montgomery: Committed as a runaway 23 July 1861 by J. D. Clarke. Released 31 December 1861 to A. Porter, Provost Marshall.

Abraham Gibbs: Committed as a runaway 23 July 1861 by W. Thompson. Released 9 February 1862 by order of the Secretary of State.

Ham Raser: Committed as a runaway 23 July 1861 by T. C. Donn. Released 9 September 1861 to W. Boniparte.

Ann: Committed as a runaway 23 July 1861 by T. C. Donn. Released 31July 1861 to G. M. Watkins.

Daniel White: Committed as a runaway 23 July 1861 by T. D. Clarke. Released 1 August 1861 to David Clemmons.

Rebecca Harris: Committed as a runaway 24 July 1861 by J. W. Barnardo. Released to James Smith.

Wilson Horrick: Committed as a runaway 25 July 1861 by J. D. Clarke. Released 5 August 1861 to Dr. Charles Duvall.

Isabella Penny: Committed as a runaway 25 July 1861 by J. W. Barnacle. Released 29 August 1861 to James N. Wynn.

Ned Geary: Committed as a runaway 25 July 1861 by B. W. Furgerson. Released 8 August 1861 to ____ Carter.

Joe: Committed for safekeeping 26 July 1861 by J. S. Hopkins. Released 25 August 1861 to J. S. Hopkins.

Handy: Committed as a runaway 26 July 1861 by J. S. Hopkins. Released 7 August 1861 to J. S. Hopkins.

John Matthews: Committed as a runaway 26 July 1861 by John D. Clarke. Released by order of the Secretary of State, date of release not legible.

John Weaver: Committed as a runaway 26 July 1861 by John D. Clarke. Died in jail 8 October 1861.

Robert Brown: Committed as a runaway 26 July 1861 by John D. Clarke. Released 30 July 1861 to Charles R. Beler.

William Hayes: Committed as a runaway 26 July 1861 by James Cull. Released 30 July 1861 to William P. Fowler.

Mary Harp: Committed as a runaway 26 July 1861 by B. W. Furgerson. Released 1 August 1861. No other data given.

Adolphus Harp: Committed as a runaway 26 July 1861 by B. W. Furgerson. Released 1 August 1861. No other data given.

Robert: Committed for safe-keeping by James Tolson 25 July 1861. Released 18 December 1861 to James Tolson.

Henry Norton: Committed as a runaway 27 July 1861 by James Cull. Released 29 July 1861 to Charles C. Brown.

Daniel F. Curtis: Committed as a runaway 27 July 1861 by N. Thompson. Released 9 February 1862 by order of the Secretary of State.

William Cole: Committed as a runaway 27 July 1861 by Lewis Whelen and Charles Walter. Released 9 December 1861 to A. Porter, Provost Marshall.

Thomas Hawkins: Committed as a runaway 27 July 1861 by Lewis Whelen and Charles Walter. Released 9 December 1861 to A. Porter, Provost Marshall.

John Hall: Committed as a runaway 28 July 1861 by P. H. King. Released 7 August 1861 to A. G. Booksey.

Jacob: Committed as a runaway 30 July 1861 by James Cull. Released 7 August 1861 to J. H. Blackford.

George Waters: Committed as a runaway 30 July 1861 by B. W. Furgerson. Released 9 August 1861 to Benjamin E. Gant.

Daniel Thompson: Committed as a runaway 30 July 1861 by B. W. Furgerson. Released 9 August 1861 to Maria F. Morton.

Samuel Matthews: Committed as a runaway 30 July 1861 by G. E. P. Matthews. Released 4 August 1861 to Resin Matthews.

Ben: Committed for safekeeping by Mrs. Little. Release notes not given.

Harrison Hopewell: Committed as a runaway 8 August 1861 by James Bull. Released 18 September 1861 as free.

Evelina Hawkins: Committed as a runaway 3 August 1861 by James Cull. Released 3 August 1861 to Jim Smith.

Rachel Hawkins: Committed as a runaway 3 August 1861 by James Cull. Released 3 August 1861 to Jim Smith.

Nathan: Committed as a runaway 4 August 1861 by Thomas C. Donn. Released 5 August 1861 to William Hill.

George Lee: Committed as a runaway 4 August 1861 by James Cull. Released 5 August 1861 to George Tolbert.

James Barnes: Committed as a runaway 4 August 1861 by B. W. Furgerson. Released 29 August 1861 to J. B. Posey.

Henry: Committed as a runaway 5 August 1861 by J. S. Hollingshead.

John Davis: Committed as a runaway 5 August 1861 by L. C. Clarke. Released 9 December 1861 to A. Porter, Provost Marshall.

Richard Shorter: Committed as a runaway 7 August 1861 by Henry Reever. Released 8 August 1861 to Robert Dick.

George Lee: Committed as a runaway 8 August 1861 by Thomas C. Donn. Released 24 September 1861 to Resin Arnold.

Henry Lee: Committed as a runaway 8 August 1861 by Thomas C. Donn. Released 24 September 1861 to Resin Arnold.

James Jackson: Committed as a runaway 8 August 1861 by Thomas C. Donn. Released 31 December 1861 to A. Porter, Provost Marshall.

Richard Olliver: Committed as a runaway 8 August 1861 by Thomas C. Donn. Released 24 October 1861 as free.

Ned Cunningham: Committed as a runaway 11 August 1861 by J. D. Clarke. Released 22 August 1861 to Withers Waller.

Henry Degs (Diggs ?) : Committed as a runaway 11 August 1861 by J. D. Clarke. Released 22 August 1861 to Withers Waller.

Beverly Pullison: Committed for safekeeping by B. F. Galleher. Released 5 August 1861 to B. F. Galleher.

Harriet: Committed as a runaway 12 August 1861 by P. McKenna. Released 15 August 1861 to Cloe Ann Soper.

Emanuel: Committed for safekeeping by Thomas C. Macgruder. Released 22 August 1861 to Thomas C. Macgruder.

John Colts: Committed as a runaway 12 August 1861 by John H. Johnson. Released 16 August to John Bowie.

Nathan Diggs: Committed as a runaway 13 August 1861 by J. D. Clarke. Released 22 August 1861 to Withers Weller.

John Diggs: Committed as a runaway 13 August 1861 by J. D. Clarke. Released 22 August 1861 to Withers Weller.

J__ Parker: Committed as a runaway 13 August 1861 by G. L. Giberson. Released 22 November 1861 to A. Porter, Provost Marshall.

Nancy Pirrer: Committed as a runaway 13 August 1861 by T. C. Donn. Released 27 November 1861 to A. Porter, Provost Marshall.

Nathan Pirrer: Committed as a runaway 13 August 1861 by T. C. Donn. Released 27 November 1861 to A. Porter, Provost Marshall.

Malinda: Committed for safekeeping by Solomon Stover 13 August 1861. Released 23 September 1861 to Benjamin Cooly.

James Thomas: Committed as a runaway 14 August 1861 by BN. W. Furgerson. Released 6 September 1861 to John Smoot.

Thomas Thompson: Committed as a runaway 13 August 1861 by J. D. Clarke. Released 18 December 1861 to A. Porter, Provost Marshall.

Clem Woodward: Committed for safekeeping by Joseph Trimble16 August 1861. Released 16 August 1861 to Joseph Trimble.

Simon: Committed as a runaway 17 August 1861 by Henry G. Murray. Released to R. Bowling. Release date not legible.

Benjamin Mattingly: Committed as a runaway 21 August 1861 by Henry G. Murray. Released to R. Bowling. Release date not legible.

William Johnson: Committed as a runaway 21 August 1861 by James Cull. Released to Dr. Peach.

George Dorsey: Committed as a runaway 21 August 1861 by P. H. King. No other notes entered.

Henry: Committed as a runaway 21 August 1861 by Henry Reaver. Released 11 September 1861 to John Lange.

Elias Wright: Committed as a runaway 25 August 1861 by T. C. Donn. Released to Thomas B. Bell.

Dick: Committed as a runaway 25 August 1861 by James Cull. Released to Mrs. Manning.

William Woodley: Committed for safekeeping by John A. Smith 27 August 1861. Released 2 September 1861 to John A. Smith.

Sandy: Committed as a runaway 25 August 1861 by James Cull. Released to John Manning.

Joseph Parr: Committed for safekeeping by A. M. Williams 26 August 1861. Released 26 August 1861 to A. M. Williams.

Robert Diggs: Committed as a runaway 28 August 1861 by Henry Reever. Released 5 September 1861 to A. Donaldson.

Mary B___: Committed as a runaway 30 August 1861 by Elias Walters. Released 31 August 1861 to George McSeeny.

Emily: Committed as a runaway 30 August 1861 by T. C. Donn. Released 31 August 1861 to P. McGill.

Thomas Carter: Committed as a runaway 31 August 1861 by T. C. Donn. Released 9 September 1861 to A. E. L. Reese.

George Patrick Henry: Committed as a runaway 31 August 1861 by J. D. Clarke. Released December 9 1861 to A. Porter, Provost Marshall.

Daniel Stokes: Committed as a runaway 2 September 1861 by R. White. Released 7 September to M. E. Gott.

John Doe: Committed for safekeeping by T. H. Shreaves 4 September 1861. Released 11 September 1861 to T. H. Shreaves.

Kitty Carpenter: Committed as a runaway 2 September 1861 by P. McKenna. Released 10 October 1861 to Robert W. Bryan.

Alfred Day: Committed as a runaway 4 September 1861 by T. C. Donn. Released 12 December 1861 to N. Miles.

James K__ Johnson: Committed as a runaway 2 September 1861 by Charles Walters. Released 8 September 1861 to _____ Bay.

Daniel Clarke: Committed for safekeeping by Ignatius Grimes 6 September 1861. Released To Thomas E. Berry.

William Hawkins: Committed as a runaway 6 September 1861 by T. C. Donn. Released 10 September 1861 to Dr. S. C. Busey.

Mary J. Washington: Committed as a runaway 7 September 1861 by B. W. Fergerson. Released 22 November 1861 as free.

John Holland: Committed as a runaway 8 September 1861 by James Cull. Released 19 September 1861 to F. N. Butler.

William Posey: Committed for safekeeping by J. Hart Burroughs 10 September 1861. Released 20 November 1861 to J. H. Mattingly.

Davis: Committed as a runaway 10 September 1861 by Robert White by order of Major Moraty of the 2nd. ___ Zouaves. Released to A. Porter, Provost Marshall.

George Anderson: Committed as a runaway 11 September 1861 by L. C. Davis. Released to F. N. Butler.

Charles Shorter: Committed as a runaway 10 September 1861 by Robert White by order of Major Moraty of the 2nd. ___ Zouaves. Released to F. N. Butler.

William Washington: Committed as a runaway 10 September 1861 by Robert White by order of Major Moraty of the 2nd. ___ Zouaves. Released to William Dangerfielder.

Shad Shorter: Committed as a runaway 10 September 1861 by Robert White by order of Major Moraty of the 2nd. ___ Zouaves. Released to William Dangerfielder.

Ned Scranton: Committed as a runaway 10 September 1861 by T. C. Donn by order of Major Moraty of the 2nd. ___ Zouaves. Released to F. N. Butler 19 September 1861.

Jesse: Committed as a runaway 12 September 1861 by F. J. Murphy. Released 13 September 1861 to F. N. Botelier.

Tom: Committed as a runaway 12 September 1861 by F. J. Murphy. Released 13 September 1861 to F. N. Botelier.

Sprigg: Committed as a runaway 12 September 1861 by F. J. Murphy. Released 13 September 1861 to F. N. Botelier.

Mat: Committed as a runaway 12 September 1861 by F. J. Murphy. Released 13 September 1861 to F. N. Botelier.

Charles: Committed as a runaway 12 September 1861 by F. J. Murphy. Released 13 September 1861 to F. N. Botelier.

Thomas Harrison: Committed as a runaway 13 September 1861 by James Cull. Released on order of the Secretary of State.

Primes: Committed as a runaway 13 September 1861 by James Cull. Released 14 September 1861 to Thomas A. Givens.

Mandy: Committed as a runaway 14 September 1861 by Charles Walters. Released 20 September 1861 to John W. Fitzhugh.

Samuel Harris: Committed as a runaway 14 September 1861 by T. C. Donn. Released

17 September 1861 to
F. N. Botlier.

Henrietta: Committed as a
runaway 15 September 1861
by Charles Walters. Released
26 September 1861 to Samuel
Pumphrey.

Isaac Young: Committed as a
runaway 14 September 1861
by T. C. Donn. Released 16
September 1861 to M.
Goddau. (Goddard?).

George Davis: Committed as a
runaway 16 September 1861
by John A. Johnson. Released
16 November 1861 to T. C.
Bruin.

John Belt: Committed as a
runaway 16 September 1861
by John A. Johnson. Released
29 November 1861 to Nimrod
Burgett.

Robert: Committed for
safekeeping by F. N. Butler16
September 1861. Released 4
October 1861 to John H.
Hunter.

Robert Brooks: Committed as a
runaway 17 September 1861
by Charles Walters. Released
5 November 1861 to William
Hunter.

Joe Henson (Hinson): Committed
as a runaway 20 September
1861 by Henry Reives.
Released 20 September 1861
to F. N. Butler.

Henry Smith: Committed for
safekeeping by William T.
Reynolds 22 September 1861.
Released 22 September 1861
to William T. Reynolds.

John: Committed as a runaway
22 September 1861 by T. C.
Donn. Released 28 September
1861 to H. B. Cashier.

Robert Fane: Committed as a
runaway 22 September 1861
by Henry Rieves. Released 9
December 1861 to A. Porter,
Provost Marshall.

Frank Wood: Committed as a
runaway 22 September 1861
by James Cull. Released to
William Jenkins.

George: Committed as a runaway
22 September 1861 by .
Released 26 November 1861
to _____ D. Bowling.

Bill Bowie: Committed as a
runaway 21 September 1861
by H. Reives. Released by
order of the Secretary of
State.

Pierce Martin: Committed as a
runaway 23 September 1861
by W. Thompson. Released to
William Miller, date unclear.

Pe_e Martin: Committed for
safekeeping by M. A. Miller
26 September 1861. Released
30 September 1861 to M. A.
Miller.

Edward: Committed as a runaway
23 September 1861 by T C.
Donn. Released to A. Porter,
Provost Marshall by order of
the Secretary of War.

Henry Butler: Committed as a
runaway 26 September 1861
by T. C. Donn. Released to
George Peters 31 September
1861.

Alfred Lyles: Committed as a
runaway 28 September 1861
by T. C. Donn. Released to
William Sheriff.

Thomas Clagett: Committed as a
runaway 28 September 1861
by Charles Walters. Released
to William M. Jones 30
September 1861.

Harriet Wilson: Committed as a runaway 28 September 1861 by T. C. Donn. Released to A. Porter, Provost Marshall 9 December 1861.

Margaritta Bean: Committed for safekeeping by Samuel C. Busey 29 September 1861. Released 9 December 1861 to Samuel C. Busey.

Alexander Posey: Committed as a runaway 30 September 1861 by T. C. Donn. Released to R. N. Darnell 12 October 1861.

Sarah Jane Brown: Committed as a runaway 30 September 1861 by T. C. Donn. Released to R. N. Darnell 12 October 1861.

Mary Ann Brown: Committed as a runaway 30 September 1861 by T. C. Donn. Released to R. N. Darnell 12 October 1861.

James Allen: Committed as a runaway 30 September 1861 by T. C. Donn. Released to R. N. Darnell 12 October 1861.

Franklin Bradly: Committed as a runaway 30 September 1861 by T. C. Donn. Released to R. N. Darnell 12 October 1861.

Richard Reed: Committed as a runaway 1 October 1861 by T. C. Donn. Released to Dr. B. J. Simms.

James Henry Wilson: Committed as a runaway 2 October 1861 by T. C. Donn. Released by order of the Secretary of State.

Robert Contee: Committed for safekeeping by Jeremiah Dudley 3 October 1861. Release date is not legible. Owner is cited as Thomas Carriet.

Albert Davis: Committed as a runaway 3 October 1861 by T. C. Donn. Released to William B_____. Date not legible.

John Davis: Committed as a runaway 4 October 1861 by T. C. Donn. Released to Thomas C. Donn.

Nathaniel Carter: Committed for safekeeping by Francis L. Borman 5 October 1861. Released to Francis L. Borman.

Joseph Clarke: Committed for safekeeping by J. W. Dain 5 October 1861. Released to J. W. Dain.

Hillery Dorsey: Committed as a runaway 6 October 1861 by James Cull. Released to Thomas Gardiner.

Joseph Smith: Committed as a runaway 6 October 1861 by T. C. Donn. No release notes entered.

Patrick Holmes: Committed as a runaway 10 October 1861 by John H. Johnson 10 October 1861. Released 16 October 1861 to William T. Sillman.

Betsy Harola: Committed for safekeeping by J. W. Snyder. Released 24 October 1861 to J. W. Snyder.

Henry Dorsey: Committed as a runaway 15 October 1861 by T. C. Donn. Released 25 November to Webb.

Jesse Wilson: Committed as a runaway 18 October 1861 by T. C. Donn. Released 9 December 1861 to William E. Cole.

Cecelia Bell & child: Committed as a runaway 18 October 1861 by T. C. Donn. Released 30 October 1861 to Pinkney Brooks.

Frank: Committed for safekeeping by F. N. Botlier 19 October 1861. Released 25 October 1861 to F. N. Botlier.

Jane: Committed for safekeeping by C. G. Gardiner. Released 25 October to C. G. Gardiner.

Carmille Jones: Committed as a runaway 24 October by D. Rowland. Released 11 November 1861 to George Thompson.

Perry Davis: Committed as a runaway 24 October by Charles Walters. Released 5 November 1861 to William Dawson.

Lucy: Committed for safekeeping by T. N. Wilson 25 October 1861. Released 6 November 1861 to T. N. Wilson.

Jake Hollins: Committed as a runaway 27 October 1861 by James Cull. Released 5 January 1862 to B. W. Marriot.

Frank Warren: Committed as a runaway 27 October 1861 by James Cull. Released 11 November to Dr. Clayton.

John Contee: Committed as a runaway 27 October 1861 by James Cull. Released to B. S. Bird.

Frank: Committed as a runaway 29 October 1861 by J. W. Barnacle. Released 27 November 1861 to J. B. Matthews.

Mary Brice: Committed as a runaway 29 October 1861 by .

Released 9 December 1861 to Ignatius Linnott.

Eliza A. West: Committed as a runaway 29 October 1861 by James Cull. Released 18 December 1861 to A. Porter, Provost Marshall.

Francis Henry: Committed as a runaway 31 October 1861 by F. J. Murphy. Released 10 December 1861 to H. R. Harris.

Henry Wiley: Committed as a runaway 31 October 1861 by F. J. Murphy. Released 15 November 1861 to J. W. Tippett.

George Beall: Committed as a runaway 31 October 1861 by F. J. Murphy. Released 20 December 1861 to Griffin Carter.

Mary Jane Brooks: Committed as a runaway 31 October 1861 by Charles Walters. Released 31 October 1861 to Basil Hall.

Henry Simms: Committed for safekeeping by John G___ Baugh 7 November 1861. Released 21 November 1861 by writ of Habeas Corpus.

Flora: Committed as a runaway 7 November 1861 by T. C. Donn. Released 28 November to Andrew Martin__.

Letetia Hall: Committed as a runaway 8 November 1861 by T. C. Donn. Released 12 November 1861 to L. Motzer.

Rosanna Gordon: Committed as a runaway 8 November 1861 by W. R. Stratton. Released

9 December 1861 to
Mary Hall.
Henry Gavenner: Committed as a
runaway 9 November 1861 by
J. W. Malloy. Released
16 November 1861 to
J. W. Crain.
Louisa Simms: Committed as a
runaway 12 November 1861
by James Cull. Released
18 November 1861 to
F. N. Botlier.
Henry Mitchell: Committed for
safekeeping by W. A. T.
Maddox. Released to
Simon Duvall.
John Haster: Committed as a
runaway 15 November 1861
by B. W. Fergerson. Released
19 November 1861 to
Charles Smith.
Jinny Lynn: Committed for
safekeeping by John C. Jones.
Released 26 November 1861
to John C. Jones.
Charles Jones: Committed as a
runaway 22 November 1861
by T. C. Donn. Released 9
December 1861 to A. Porter,
Provost Marshall.
Betsy Harold: Committed for
safekeeping by J. W. Snyder.
Released 30 November 1861
to J. W. Snyder.
Thomas Coleman: Committed as a
runaway 26 November 1861
by T. C. Donn. Released
12 December 1861 to
F. J. Lybott.
Thomas Swann: Committed as a
runaway 26 November 1861
by T. C. Donn. Released 28
November 1861 to
A. Porter, Provost Marshall.
_____ **Middleton:** Committed as
a runaway 26 November 1861

by T. C. Donn. Released 28
November 1861 to A. Porter,
Provost Marshall.
John Hains: Committed as a
runaway 26 November 1861
by T. C. Donn. Released
28 November 1861 to
A. Porter, Provost Marshall.
Julia Middleton: Committed as a
runaway 26 November 1861
by T. C. Donn. Released
28 November 1861 to
A. Porter, Provost Marshall.
Elizabeth Swann: Committed as a
runaway 26 November 1861
by T. C. Donn. Released
28 November 1861 to A.
Porter, Provost Marshall.
Minta Middleton: Committed as a
runaway 17 December 1861
by J. N. Pearson. Released 30
May 1862 to John Smith.
Robert Bell: Committed for
safekeeping by T. C. Donn 20
December 1861. Released
21 December 1861 to
Griffin Carter.
Henry Young: Committed for
safekeeping by T. C. Donn 20
December 1861. Released
21 December 1861 to
Griffin Carter.
James Johnson: Committed as a
runaway 25 December 1861
by B. W. Fergerson. Released
30 December to
Margaret A. Devar.
James Coger: Committed as a
runaway 2 January 1862 by
Henry G. Murray. Released
11 January to William
Stockett.
Hillery Chase: Committed as a
runaway by 2 January 1862.
Released 8 January 1862 to
F. B. Edelin.

William Griffith: Committed as a runaway 3 January 1862 by James Cull. Released 6 January 1862 to John W. Badu.

John Selvey: Committed as a runaway 3 January 1862 by James Cull. Released 9 January 1862 to John Summers.

John Loks (Lock/Locke): Committed as a runaway 3 January 1862 by James Cull. Released 10 January 1862 to William B. Perry.

Abraham Edwards: Committed as a runaway 8 January 1862 by T. C. Donn. Released 9 February by order of the Secretary of State.

Lloyd Mason: Committed for safekeeping by Charles Waters. Released by order of the Secretary of State 9 January 1862.

John Jackson: Committed as a runaway 8 January 1862 by A. G. Murray. Released 8 January 1862 to ____ Martin.

Charles: Committed as a runaway 17 January 1862 by T. C. Donn. Released to Thomas J. Inglehart.

Dick: Committed as a runaway 17 January 1862 by T. C. Donn. Released to Thomas J. Inglehart.

Jacob: Committed as a runaway 17 January 1862 by T. C. Donn. Released to Thomas J. Inglehart.

Henry: Committed as a runaway 17 January 1862 by T. C. Donn. Released to Thomas J. Inglehart.

Mary ____: Committed as a runaway January 1862 by H. G. Murray. Released 27 January 1862 to Henry Ball.

Robert Lanham: Committed as a runaway January 1862 by H. G. Murray. Released 27 January 1862 to Henry Ball.

____ Brooks: Committed as a runaway 27 January 1862 by N. G. Murray. Released to R. O. Mulligan.

Robert Brooks: Committed as a runaway 27 January 1862 by N. G. Murray. Released to R. O. Mulligan.

Lonn: Committed as a runaway 28 January 1862 by T. C. Donn. Released 29 January 1862 to F. N. Botlier.

Thomas Jefferson: Committed as a runaway 28 January 1862 by N. G. Murray. Released 17 February 1862 to William O. Reeder

Henry Fisher: Committed as a runaway 28 January 1862 by N. G. Murray. Released by order of the Secretary of State.

Tyler: Committed as a runaway 30 January 1862 by T. C. Donn. Released to F. N. Botlier

Martha: Committed as a runaway 30 January 1862 by T. C. Donn. Released by order of the Provost Marshall.

Samuel Dorsey: Committed as a runaway 31 January 1862 by H. G. Murray. Released to J. D. Bowling.

Allen: Committed as a runaway 2 February 1862 by T. C.

Donn. Released to
F. N. Botlier.

Abram Taylor: Committed as a
runaway 2 February 1862 by
Charles Walter. Released to
Peter Wheeler.

J. H. Brown alias J. H. Thomas:
Committed as a runaway 3
February 1862 by James Cull.
Released to J. D. Bowling.

___ **Brown:** Committed as a
runaway 3 February 1862 by
James Cull. Released to
F. N. Botlier.

John Grant: Committed as a
runaway 3 February 1862 by
James Cull. Released to
F. N. Botlier.

William Hall: Committed as a
runaway 5 February 1862 by
F. J. Murphy. Released to J.
W. Allen.

Henry Williams: Committed as a
runaway 5 February 1862 by
J. H. Johnson. Discharged by
order of the Secretary of
State.

Sally Fisherman: Committed as a
runaway 5 February 1862 by
James Cull. Released to W.
W. Liles (Lyles?).

Nat Compton: Committed as a
runaway 7 February 1862 by
G. L. Giberson. Released to
Thomas E. Barry.

Washington Robinson:
Committed as a runaway
7 February 1862 by G. L.
Giberson. Released to
Thomas E. Barry.

Harry Harrison: Committed as a
runaway 7 February 1862.
Released 21 February to
William Ridenour.

___ **Tyler:** Committed as a
runaway 9 February 1862 by

T. C. Donn. Released
12 February 1861 to
Thomas Marshall.

Frank: Committed as a runaway 9
February 1862. Released 15
February 1862 to Dr. Lauser.

Amelia Tyler: Committed as a
runaway 16 February 1862 by
T. C. Donn. Released to the
Provost Marshall 19 February
1862.

Elnora Diggs: Committed as a
runaway 16 February 1862 by
T. C. Donn. Released to C.
Kemble (Kimble) 18 February
1862.

William Bell: Committed as a
runaway 24 February 1862 by
T. C. Donn. Released to
Robert Marshall 26 February
1862.

Mary Bell: Committed as a
runaway 24 February 1862 by
T. C. Donn. Released to Selby
Scaggs 26 February 1862.

Edward Bell: Committed as a
runaway 27 February 1862 by
T. C. Donn. Released to Selby
Scaggs 27 February 1862.

Daniel Williams: Committed as a
runaway 27 February 1862 by
H. G. Murray. Released to
himself.

Dick Prine/Price: Committed as a
runaway 27 February 1862 by
T. C. Donn. Released by order
of the Secretary of State.

Aquila Mosley: Committed as a
runaway 27 February 1862 by
T. C. Donn. Released by order
of the Secretary of State.

Lewis: Committed as a runaway
3 March 1862 by T. C. Donn.
Released to Wire & Kemble.

Washington Watts: Committed as
a runaway 3 March 1862 by

T. C. Donn. Released to Wire & Kemble.

Jasper Thomas Williams: Committed as a runaway 3 March 1862. Released to himself.

Mary L. Simpson: Committed as a runaway 10 March 1862 by T. C. Donn. Released to William Allen.

James Harrison: Committed as a runaway by T. C. Donn. No release notes.

Ben, property of Charles Clark: Committed as a runaway March 1862 by T. C. Donn. Released by order of the Secretary of State.

Edward Francis: Committed as a runaway March 1862 by J. D. Clarke. Released to William A. Bass/Boss.

Charles Francis: Committed as a runaway March 1862 by J. D. Clarke. Released to William A. Bass/Boss.

George Francis: Committed as a runaway March 1862 by J. D. Clarke. Released to William A. Bass/Boss.

____ **Turner:** Committed as a runaway 20 March 1862 by T. C. Donn. Released 29 March 1862 to John Wise.

George Washington: Committed as a runaway 20 March 1862 by T. C. Donn. Released 29 March 1862 to John Wise.

Nace Barnes: Committed as a runaway 20 March 1862 by T. C. Donn. Released 29 March 1862 to William S. Offutt.

Charlotte Oliver: Committed as a runaway 25 March 1862 by T. C. Donn. Released 7 April 1862 to Robert McGee.

Harriet Jackson: Committed as a runaway 25 March 1862 by T. C. Donn. Released to Dr. Cook.

Asbury Jackson: Committed as a runaway 25 March 1862 by T. C. Donn. Released to Dr. Cook.

Harriet Wood: Committed as a runaway 4 April 1862 by James Cull. Released to William Bowie (Mrs.?)_.

Martha Wood, infant: Committed as a runaway 4 April 1862 by James Cull. Released to William Bowie (Mrs.?)_.

Claggett Wood: Committed as a runaway 4 April 1862 by James Cull. Released to William Bowie (Mrs.?)).

Frank Wood: Committed as a runaway 4 April 1862 by James Cull. Released to William Bowie (Mrs.?)).

Jacob Wood: Committed as a runaway 4 April 1862 by James Cull. Released to William Bowie (Mrs.?)).

Alexander: Committed as a runaway 4 April 1862 by T. C. Donn. Released by order of the Secretary of State.

John Chase: Committed as a runaway 9 April March 1862 by T. C. Donn. Released to George L. Hodden.

Thomas Childs: Committed as a runaway 9 April March 1862 by T. C. Donn. Released to George L. Hodden.

Amanda Curtis: Committed as a runaway 5 April March 1862 by T. C. Donn. Released to M. Morehead.

Actions in the U. S. District Court for the District of Columbia in Reference to Fugitive Slaves

15 May 1862.
Margaret A. White Smoot, Montgomery Co filed a petition for warrant of arrest as a fugitive slave against **Tilghman Rivers.**
James E. S. Holloday, Prince George's Co filed a Petition for warrant of arrest as fugitive slaves against **James Clark, and Phillip Clark.**
Benjamin R. White of Montgomery Co. filed a petition for warrant of arrest as a fugitive slave against **Samuel Anderson.** 21 May 1862 Deposition attesting to ownership of Anderson is filed by Daniel White, brother of Benjamin White.
21 May 1862 Order remanding Samuel Anderson to owner Benjamin R. White is issued.
21 May 1862: Order permitting removal of Samuel Anderson to Maryland is issued.
Benjamin R. White of Montgomery Co. filed a petition for warrant of arrest as a fugitive slave against **Jim Warren.**
John E. Bowie of Prince Georges Co filed a petition for warrant of arrest as a fugitive slave against **George Dyson, age 51 0r 52, a.k.a. Gassaway.**
John E. Bowie of Prince Georges Co filed a petition for warrant of arrest as a fugitive slave against **Nora Ross.**
Thomas Cross of Prince George's Co filed a petition for warrant of arrest as a fugitive slave against **John Brogden, and Louisa Allen.**
George Duvall of Prince George's Co. files a deposition affirming the ownership of Louisa Allen by Thomas Cross, indicating that Louisa Allen was given to Thomas Cross by his grandfather.
Order remanding Louisa Allen to owner Thomas Cross and permitting her removal to Maryland is issued.
Dr. Charles Duvall of Prince George's Co., Md. filed a petition for warrant of arrest as a fugitive slaves against **Tom Chesley, Lee Chesley.**
Dennis Duvall of Prince George's Co. filed a petition for warrant of arrest as a fugitive slave against **Basil West, John Sprigg, Jacob Johnson, Lloyd West, John Jackson, Lucy Johnson, Bill Johnson, 8, Lewis**

Johnson, 10, Frank Johnson, 8, Josephine Johnson, 3[10], Maria Brogden, Dick, Laura, and Harriet Sprigg. George W. Duvall, son of Dennis Duvall files a deposition attesting to the ownership of Harriet Sprigg, Maria Brogden, Dick, and Laura by Dennis Duvall.

16 May 1862: Order remanding **Basil West, John Sprigg, Jacob Johnson, Lloyd West, John Jackson, Lucy Johnson, Bill Jackson, 8, Lewis Johnson, 10, Frank Johnson, 8, Josephine Johnson, 3, Maria Brogden, Dick, Laura, and Harriet Sprigg[11]** to Dennis Duvall and permitting their return to Maryland is issued.

12 June 1862: Order remanding **John Jackson and Bill Jackson** to Dennis Duvall and permitting their return to Maryland is issued.

George W. Duvall filed a petition for warrant of arrest as fugitive slaves against **John Johnson, Eli Harrison, Jim Hall, and Jack Hall.**

16 May 1862

Oratio Claggett filed a petition for warrant of arrest as a fugitive slave against **Rezin Addison[12], and Lloyd Magruder.**

19May 1862: Order remanding Addison & Magruder to Claggett and permitting their return to Maryland is issued.

Richard Darnell of Prince George's Co. filed a petition for warrant of arrest as a fugitive slave against **Mary Jane Brown.**

William H. Offutt of Montgomery County, Md. filed a petition for warrant of arrest as a fugitive slave against **Alfred Smith**

.   21 May 1862: Order remanding Alfred Smith to William H. Offut issued.

17 May 1862

Lewis Magruder of Prince George's Co. filed a petition for warrant of arrest as a fugitive slaves against **William Wight, Elizabeth Taylor/ Dorsey/Burr, Ellen Simms, Jane Simms, and Harriet Simms.**

---

[10] Bill, Lewis, Frank and Josephine are children of Lucy Johnson.

[11] Children of Maria Brogden.

[12] Purchased from the estate of Thomas Scott.

Bill of Sale dated 1 December 1857 from Bernard M.
Campbell to Lewis Magruder of Elizabeth Dorsey is
admitted as evidence 20 May 1862.

John G. Mitchell of Prince George's Co. filed a petition for
warrant of arrest as a fugitive slave against **Nathan Bell**.

John Higgins filed a petition for warrant of arrest as fugitive
slaves against **Charles Sewell, Judson Sewell, Sophy
Bartlett, and William, son of Sophy.**

Joseph M. Parker (Packer?)of Prince George's Co. filed a
petition for warrant of arrest as a fugitive slave against
John Bevins and Robert Green.

Joseph Manning of Prince George's Co. filed a petition for
warrant of arrest as fugitive slaves against **Richard
Bowie and Ann Maria Harris.**

Samuel J. Birkett of Prince George's Co. filed a petition for
warrant of arrest as a fugitive slave against **John Ross**.

19 May 1862

Felder Magruder of Prince George's Co. filed a petition for
warrant of arrest as a fugitive slave against **Anthony
Crawford.**

Robert Dicks of Montgomery Co. filed a petition for warrant
of arrest as fugitive slaves against **Perry, Jane, John,
Tom and Margaret.**

Order to remand **Perry, Jane, John, Tom and Margaret** to
Robert Dicks is issued.

Benjamin Padgett of Prince George's Co. filed a petition for
warrant of arrest as fugitive slaves against **Nat Brown,
Ben Tasker, Lewis Tasker, John Tasker, Ned Tasker,
Elias Tasker, Lucy, Barbara Daniel, Amelia, Rachel,
Mary Jane and George.**

James E. Jones gives a deposition in support of the
claim of Benjamin Padgett.

Order to remand Lucy, Barbara, Daniel, Rachel, George,
Mary Jane to Benjamin Padgett is issued.

William Mackall, Ann Arundel Co. filed a petition for warrant
of arrest as a fugitive slave against **John Hobbs, Joseph
Hobbs, Virgie Tasker, Henry Brooks, and
Washington Hutton.**

Fayette Ball of Ann Arundel Co. filed a petition for warrant of
arrest as fugitive slaves against **Daniel Carroll and
Lewis ___.**

John A. Iglehart of Ann Arundel Co. filed a petition for
warrant of arrest as a fugitive slaves against **William
Tilghman, and George Stevens.**[13]
Order to deliver William Tilghman and
George Stevens to Inglehart is issued 9 June 1862.
Maria T. Doll of Prince George's Co. filed a petition for
warrant of arrest as fugitive slaves against **Frank, Kitty,
Ann, Isabelle, Jane, Peter, Jeffrey.**
Nathaniel Claggett of Montgomery Co. filed a petition for
warrant of arrest as fugitive slaves against **Johnson
Brown, Almira Smith, John, William, and Charles.**[14]
James Waring of Prince George's Co. filed a petition for
warrant of arrest as fugitive slaves against **Joe Jones,
Patrick Steward, Washington Jackson, Daniel
Calvert, Richard Jones, ____ Stewart, William Jones,
Edward Johnson, Stephen Williams, Annie Calvert,
Catherine Calvert, Amelia Jones, Annie Jones, Sallie,
Bitt, Jim, and Caroline Jopping.**
John Mitchell of Prince George's Co. filed a petition for
warrant of arrest as fugitive slaves against **James
Carroll, Tom Duffin, Frederick Chitterson, John
Harkley, Nancy Chitterson, mother of Frederick.**
John T. Hardy of Howard Co. filed a petition for warrant of
arrest as a fugitive slave against **Charles Davis.**
Order to remand **Charles Davis** to John T. Hardy is
issued.
21 May 1862
Order remanding **Elizabeth Dorsey** to Lewis Magruder and
permitting her return to Maryland is issued.
22 May 1862
The Court ordered the U. S. Marshall to deliver **William
Henry Burns**, fugitive slave to Lewis Magruder.
14 April 1863
William F. Holliday of Ann Arundel Co. filed a petition for
warrant of arrest as fugitive slaves against **Eliza and her
children, John, William, Benjamin, and Mary.**
J. G. Kent of Calvert Co. filed a petition for warrant of arrest
as a fugitive slave against Decker Giles.

---

[13] Purchased from the estate of William Wooten.
[14] John, William, and Charles are children of A. Smith.

Charles R. Belt, agent of Ellen U. Belt of Calvert Co. filed a petition for warrant of arrest as a fugitive slave against **Dick Stevenson**.

Walter A. Edelin of Prince George's Co. filed a petition for warrant of arrest as fugitive slaves against **Harriet Davis, and Frank Davis.**

> Warrant for the arrest of Harriet and Frank Davis issued 14 April 1863.

16 April 1863

George W. Watkins of Montgomery Co. filed a petition for warrant of arrest as fugitive slaves against **John Edwards, Sarah Edwards, Richard Edwards, and Charity Edwards.**

20 April 1863

George W. Duvall of Prince George's Co. filed a petition for warrant of arrest as fugitive slaves against **Robert Harrison, Andrew Hall, and Thomas Tolson.**

Frederick L. Dent of Charles Co. filed a petition for warrant of arrest as a fugitive slave against **William.**

George H. Hunter of Prince George's Co. filed a petition for warrant of arrest as fugitive slaves against **Paul Briscoe, Edward Nichols, and, Sophia Beall.**

21 April 1863

Cornelius F. Miller filed a petition for warrant of arrest as a fugitive slave against **Thomas Docket.**

Leonard H. Canter of St. Mary's Co. filed a petition for warrant of arrest as fugitive slaves against **Ned Chew and Buck.**

Richard Crownsvill Jr. of Ann Arundel Co. filed a petition for warrant of arrest as fugitive slaves against **Basle Todd, Peregrine Hooper, Martha Hooper, Frank, and Maria.**

22 April 1863

Samuel R. Bird of Calvert Co. filed a petition for warrant of arrest as fugitive slaves against **Elijah Hawkins, Henry Dorsey, Jane Dorsey[15], James Downey, Nick Boston, John Jones, and Nick Jones.**

> *23 April 1863*
>
> Samuel R. Bird disclaims ownership of all of the above slaves with the exception of Elijah Hawkins, and

---

[15] Wife of Henry Dorsey.

requests that the arrest warrant be limited to Elijah Hawkins.

James P. Martin of Baltimore Co. filed a petition for warrant of arrest as fugitive slaves against **Rebecca Howard, and her son, James Howard.**

Artemis Riggs of Montgomery Co. filed a petition for warrant of arrest as fugitive slaves against **Laura Hall, Ellen Dorsey, and the two children of Ellen Dorsey, Mary Lizzie, and Ida.**

William Clarke of Prince George's Co. filed a petition for warrant of arrest as fugitive slaves against **Clem, Sophia, Kitty, Isabel, Amanda, Statia, Michael, and Ernest a child of Isabel.**

29 April 1863

Samuel B. Anderson of Montgomery Co. filed a petition for warrants of arrest as fugitive slaves against **Fannie, Laura, Ismal, and Robert.**

INDEX

Adams, Evan, 97
Adams, John, 4, 5, 6, 7, 10, 13,
  14, 15, 19, 22, 25, 26, 30,
  31, 35, 41
Adams, Robert, 95
Addison, Bill, 57
Addison, Elizabeth, 1
Addison, John, 54, 59
Addison, Rederick, 94
Addison, Rezin, 111
Agee, William, 56
Alestock John, 92
Alexander, Arthur, 20, 53
Alexander, C., 2, 24, 33, 55
Alfred, William, 55
Allen, Charles, 73
Allen, Henry, 7
Allen, James, 4, 104
Allen, John, 61
Allen, Louisa, 110
Allen, William, 109
Allnutt, Lawrence, 28
Allnutt, William W., 61
Ambush, Stephen, 29
Anderson, Charles, 41
Anderson, Dick, 67
Anderson, George, 102
Anderson, James, 94
Anderson, Jane, 66
Anderson, John W., 45
Anderson, Samuel, 110
Anderson, Samuel B., 90, 115
Anderson, Thomas, 48
Andrews, T. P., 10
Anthony, George T., 88
Appleton, Edward, 54
Armstrong, Bill, 63
Arnold, Frank, 34
Arnold, Resin, 92, 99
Athey, P. W., 27
Atkins, John, 6
Atkinson, Frederick, 83
Aver, Thomas, 56
Badecourt, George, 13
Baden, Basil, 63
Baden, Thomas E., 41

Badu, John W., 107
Bailey, John, 54, 73
Baily, Elizabeth, 37
Baker, David, 26
Baker, Elbert, 44, 49
Baker, Emily, 31
Baker, Maria, 52
Baldwin, Thomas, 16
Ball, E. B., 22
Ball, Edward, 61
Ball, Henry, 107
Ball, Joseph, 76
Ball, O. B., 5
Ball, Thomas, 6
Baltimore, Anthony, 61
Banks, Henry, 40, 95
Banks, Tilghman, 74
Baptist, John, 93
Barber, Margaret, 38
Barbour, Henry, 87
Barbour, Phillip, 53
Barbour, S. A., 75
Barker, J. W., 27
Barker, Margaret, 40
Barker, William, 88
Barnach, William H., 22, 34,
  40
Barnell, George H., 97
Barnes, Frank, 80
Barnes, Henry, 51, 57
Barnes, James, 99
Barnes, Lewis, 23
Barnes, Milly, 19
Barnes, Nace, 79, 109
Barnet, Richard, 38
Barr, Henry J., 95
Barry, David, 60, 66
Barry, Sophia, 35
Bartholo, L. S., 83
Bartlett, Sophy, 112
Barton, Emily, 40
Bass/Boss, William A., 109
Bassy, Thomas, 15
Bates, Fred, 32
Batson, Daniel, 54, 58
Batson, Mary, 32

Bauce, Thomas, 62
Beal, Ann E., 5
Beale, 26, 38
Beale, Joe, 26
Beale, Lloyd, L., 6
Beall, B., 29, 31, 33, 44, 59
Beall, B., 5
Beall, Bailey, 4
Beall, George, 105
Beall, R. D., 21
Beall, Thomas J., 31
Beall, Z. B., 28, 29
Bealle, Charles R., 17
Beams, Alfred, 60
Beans, Charles`, 6
Beard, Capt. Thomas W., 39
Beatle, George F., 17
Beck, 36, 39, 40, 50
Beck, J. W., 2
Beck, Samuel J., 8
Beckett, Bill, 85
Beckett, Richard, 34
Beckman, Sarah J., 53
Becky, Samuel J., 8
Beler, Charles R., 98
Bell, Alfred, 34
Bell, Amos, 2
Bell, Amos., 2
Bell, Benjamin, 2
Bell, Cecila, 105
Bell, Chris, 82
Bell, David, 40
Bell, Edward, 83, 108
Bell, Jane, 82
Bell, Jenny, 82
Bell, John, 16, 53, 79
Bell, Mary, 108
Bell, Nathan, 112
Bell, Otho, 1
Bell, Patrick, 19
Bell, Robert, 106
Bell, Sarah, 86
Bell, Thomas B., 101
Bell, William, 108
Bell, William J., 19
Bell, Z, 4, 88
Bell, Z. B., 1
Belt, A. C., 4

Belt, C. R., 32
Belt, Charles R., 114
Belt, Ellen U., 114
Belt, J. B., 32
Belt, John, 103
Belt, John L., 29
Belt, Stephen, 72
Belt, W. Seaton, 42
Bennett, 19
Benson, William, 47
Benson, William H., 45, 75
Bernard, W. E. F., 1
Berrett, Joseph, 62
Berry, A. B., 31, 44, 45, 50, 53, 82
Berry, A. L., 25
Berry, Alfred M., 40
Berry, Charles, 33
Berry, Samuel T., 21
Berry, Thomas E., 81, 97, 101
Berry, Zack, 83
Bersley, Joseph, 77
Besom, William, 93
Bessey, John, 2
Bett, Addison, 50
Bettinger, 22
Bettinger, John, 22
Bevins, John, 112
Bind, William, 11
Bingham, Arthur, 79
Bingham, Harrison, 71
Bingham, Henry, 79
Birch, James H., 45, 49
Birch, Samuel, 49
Bird, John, 44
Bird, Samuel R. James P. Martin, 114, 115
Bird, Thomas R., 49
Black Hawk, 56
Black, George, 54
Blackson, Nace, 73
Blackstone, John, 67
Blackwell, Teresa, 17
Bladen, Richard, 39
Blair, Reuben, 50
Bland, William H., 14
Blandford, S., 25
Blaney Bingham, 10

Brooks, John A., 26
Brooks, Joseph, 12
Brooks, Judson, 2
Brooks, Mark, 79
Brooks, Martha, 59
Brooks, Mary Jane, 82, 105
Brooks, Nathan, 73
Brooks, Nathaniel, 67
Brooks, Robert, 103, 107
Brooks, Saulsbury, 45
Brooks, Sena, 17
Brooks, Sylvester, 55
Brooks, T. R., 3
Brooks, Tompson R., 9
Brown, Adam, 61
Brown, Basil, 48, 70
Brown, Benjamin, 93
Brown, Bill, 90
Brown, Calvert, 31
Brown, Charles, 32, 78
Brown, Charles C., 98
Brown, E., 21
Brown, Edward, 89
Brown, Elizabeth, 77
Brown, Ellen, 56
Brown, Henry, 94
Brown, Hillery, 91
Brown, J. H., 108
Brown, James, 2, 34
Brown, Joe, 48
Brown, John, 40, 45, 49, 93
Brown, John H., 96
Brown, Johnson, 113
Brown, Joseph, 8, 33
Brown, Margaret, 78
Brown, Maria, 80
Brown, Martha, 55
Brown, Mary Ann, 104
Brown, Mary Jane, 111
Brown, Nace, 22, 25
Brown, Nat, 112
Brown, Nelly, 47
Brown, Patsy, 48
Brown, Paul, 24
Brown, Phillip, 60
Brown, Richard, 72, 81
Brown, Robert, 3, 46, 51, 84,
   95, 98

Brown, Rosetta, 77
Brown, Sarah Jane, 104
Brown, Thomas, 8
Brown, Walter F., 37
Brown, William, 71, 95, 96
Browne, Bob, 10
Browne, Frank, 11
Bruce, Phillip, 4
Bruce, Thomas, 95
Bruin, Joseph, 42
Bruton, M. B., 1
Bryan, 11, 89, 101
Bryan, Robert W., 101
Bryant, Louisa, 87
Bryer, D. R., 22
Bucher, J. M., 13
Buckhead, 24
Buckley, J. S., 1, 26, 28
Buckley, John T., 32
Bud, Mary, 44
Bulger, Ann M., 54
Bunch, Henry, 8
Bunche, John C., 30
Burgess, Charles, 85
Burgett, Nimrod, 103
Burk, James, 38
Burke, John W., 92
Burnet, John, 53
Burns, William Henry, 113
Burr, R. R., 7
Burroughs, J. W., 50
Burwell, Paris, 37
Busey, Samuel C., 104
Bush, Andrew, 93
Bush, Bob, 82
Bush, Caroline, 48
Bush, Frederick H., 92
Butches, John, 17
Butler, Ben, 74
Butler, Benjamin, 68
Butler, Billy, 11
Butler, Francis M., 64
Butler, Frank, 92
Butler, Henry, 86, 103
Butler, Jack, 93
Butler, John, 70
Butler, John H., 65, 68, 96
Butler, Matilda, 35

Curtis, Henry, 11
Curtis, Jesse, 55
Curtis, John, 77, 86
Cury, Ben, 52
Dade, Thomas, 60
Daley, 20
Daley, Frances, 20
Dangerfield, Henry, 48
Dangerfield, William, 102
Danson, George W., 72
Darcey, Edward L., 5
Darnell, Benjamin, 34
Darnell, R. N., 31, 56, 88, 104
Darnell, Richard, 111
Darnes, Robert, 45
Dasher, Bill, 82
Davidson, George, 58
Davidson, Thomas, 72, 96
Davis Henry, 7, 52
Davis, Albert, 104
Davis, Ann Maria, 73
Davis, Benjamin, 40
Davis, Charles, 113
Davis, Frank, 114
Davis, George, 103
Davis, Hariet, 9, 114
Davis, Harriet, 9, 114
Davis, Henry, 52
Davis, Jacob, 94
Davis, Jane, 3, 13
Davis, John, 9, 10, 21, 22, 26,
    32, 37, 49, 50, 66, 70, 80,
    86, 92, 99, 104
Davis, Lloyd, 83
Davis, Perry, 105
Davis, Rosetta, 31, 45
Davis, Thomas, 61
Dawson, 19, 24, 105
Dawson, William, 19, 24, 105
Day, Alfred, 101
Day, Peter, 77
Day, Thomas, 29
Dean, John, 71
Dean, John T. W., 55
Degs, Henry, 100
Deitley, J. D., 33
Delany, Charles, 73
Dent, Frederick L., 114

Devar, Margaret A., 106
DeVaughn, Sam, 67
Deveal, John, 44
Dick, Robert, 46, 99, 112
Dickerson, N. C., 24
Diggs, Elnora, 108
Diggs, Elvira, 40
Diggs, George, 3, 15, 40, 75,
    95
Diggs, George F, 28
Diggs, Harris, 58
Diggs, James, 95
Diggs, John, 100
Diggs, Joseph, 67
Diggs, Lethe, 51
Diggs, Letty, 47
Diggs, Levy/Levi, 2
Diggs, Lewis, 44
Diggs, Nathan, 100
Diggs, Richard, 77, 96
Diggs, Robert, 26, 101
Dikes, Boswell, 62
Dimes, George, 74
Dinen, John, 11
Dixon, Aloysons, 88
Dixon, John H., 16
Dodge, Allen, 97
Dodson, Cynthia Ann, 58
Dodson, Elizabeth, 53
Dodson, Harriet, 76
Doe, John, 101
Dogans, Jim, 90
Donaldson, 30, 86, 101
Donn, John W., 22
Doras, Joseph, 77
Dormas, Henry, 83
Dorsey, Allen, 91
Dorsey, Edward, 77
Dorsey, Elizabeth, 112, 113
Dorsey, Ellen, 115
Dorsey, George, 101
Dorsey, Henry, 104, 115
Dorsey, Hillery, 104
Dorsey, Jack, 82
Dorsey, James, 39
Dorsey, Jane, 115
Dorsey, John H., 19
Dorsey, Maria, 84

Farmer, Charles, 97
Fendall, Phillip R., 5
Fender, Bill, 63
Fennell, Horatio, 21
Fenwick, 11, 48
Fenwick, Ann, 48
Fergerson, John R., 21
Fidden, Margaret, 6
Fields, John Henry, 20
Fisher, Henry, 107
Fisherman, Sally, 108
Fitzhugh, John W., 102
Fleming, A., 5, 22
Fletcher, 18, 33, 46, 47, 50, 52
Fletcher, Charles, 50
Fletcher, Eliza, 46
Fletcher, John, 18, 52
Fletcher, Robert, 47, 52
Flint, James, 34
Florence, J. E., 30
Foot, Solomon, 97
Forber, J. J., 25
Forbes, J. J., 25
Forbes, James J., 44
Ford, N. Francis, 49
Ford, Walter, 97
Ford, William, 97
Forrest, Bladen, 57
Forrest, William, 77
Fortwell, John R., 8
Fortwell, John R., 8
Fouke, Isaac, 52
Fowler, Henderson, 45
Fowler, James, 45
Fowler, James J., 62
Fowler, William P., 98
Francis, Charles, 109
Francis, Edward, 109
Francis, George, 109
Frank Green, 64
Franklin, Alfred, 89
Franklin, James, 97
Franklin, Kitty, 35, 47
Frasier, James W., 69
Frazier, Kitty, 18
Freaser, Kitty, 5
Frederick, Benjamin, 45
Frederick, Stephen, 92

Freeman, Howard, 53
Freeman, James, 97
French, Jacob, 45
Frier, John, 31
Fronike, Richard, 7
Fronike, Susan, 7
Fulton, J. B. H., 25
Furgison, William, 73
Gairy, Thomas H., 64
Gaither, George, 96
Gallaway, 20, 63
Gallaway, Dennis, 63
Gallaway, Jonas, 20
Gammel, John, 49
Gannan, Edmund, 7
Gannon, Edmund, 8
Gannon, Edward, 8
Gant, Andrew, 69
Gant, Benjamin E., 99
Gant, Jacob, 9, 21, 36
Gant, Tom, 76
Gantt, C. L., 3
Gantt, Jacob, 21, 36
Gantt, Rezin, 60
Gantt, Richard F., 22
Gardiner, Thomas, 104
Gardner, Alfred, 56
Garner, Primus, 41, 45
Garner, Princes, 62
Garon, Catherine`, 91
Garrett, Anthony, 14
Garrison, John K., 34
Gassaway, Charity, 60
Gassaway, Lewis, 60
Gassaway, William F., 4
Gasttridge, John, 2
Gavenner, Henry, 106
Geary, Ned, 98
Genery, Adela, 43
Gent, Servent, 92
George T. Richards, 6, 7, 12, 25
Gibbs, Abraham, 98
Gibbs, Henry, 44
Gibson, 19, 61, 82
Gibson, Henry, 19
Gibson, John, 82
Gibson, Joshua, 61

Givens, Thomas A., 102
Godfrey, Ellen, 43
Goines, John, 16
Goldsmith, Maria, 95
Gordan, Rose, 74
Gorden, E., 32
Gordon, Charles, 43, 96
Gordon, Jerry, 52
Gordon, Letha, 55
Gordon, Rosan, 54
Gordon, Rosanna, 45, 105
Gosman, J. P., 2, 48
Gould, Ellen, 51
Grady, David, 60
Graham, Edward, 56
Grant, John, 108
Gray, Ann Maria, 32
Gray, Henry, 39
Gray, James G., 76
Gray, James L., 4
Gray, Lloyd, 40
Gray, Priscilla, 13
Gray, Thomas, 82
Gredy, John, 84
Green, Bennett, 19
Green, Bill, 73
Green, Duff, Jr., 26
Green, George, 90
Green, Henry, 34
Green, Jane, 36
Green, John, 37, 60
Green, Margaret, 16
Green, Sandy, 53
Green, Sarah, 38
Greenleaf, Washington, 48
Grier, Austin, 19
Griffin, Conner, 96
Griffin, Howard, 96
Griffin, Jesse, 6
Griffith, Walters, 70
Griffith, William, 51, 107
Grimes, John A., 45
Grimes, Thomas, 84
Gross, Nace, 53
Gross, Robert, 87
Gross, William, 85
Guinn, William H., 17
Gunnell, William, 71

Gwynn, James E., 43
Gwynn, John, 43
H. B. Goodwin, 10
Hackey, William, 46
Hadden, Harry, 55
Hagen, Rosetta, 11
Hains, John, 106
Haley, Charles, 24
Hall, Anderson, 91
Hall, Andrew, 114
Hall, Charles, 91
Hall, Daniel, 45
Hall, Francis, 39
Hall, Francis M., 85
Hall, Frank, 25
Hall, Jim, 62, 111
Hall, Joe, 24
Hall, John, 70, 82, 99
Hall, Laura, 115
Hall, Letetia, 105
Hall, Mary, 54, 106
Hall, Mary Ann, 8
Hall, Peter, 65
Hall, R. F., 25
Hall, Richard F., 24
Hall, william, 54, 108
Hall, William, 4, 54, 108
Hall, William H., 7
Hamilton, John C., 74
Hamilton, John T., 25
Hamilton, William, 42
Hammond, Mary, 71
Hampkins, 15
Hampkins, Molly, 15
Hancocke, 10
Hancocke, John B., 10
Handon, 29
Handon, Thomas, 29
Handy, 9, 10, 14, 17, 41, 47,
    48, 51, 98
Handy, E. G., 9, 10, 14, 17, 41,
    47
Haney, Lydia, 87
Hannah, 10, 14, 22, 73, 85
Hanne, Susan, 71
Hanson, Richard, 54
Hanson, Sandy, 74
Hanson, Thomas, 76

Harden, Richard, 79
Hardesty, George W., 51
Hardin, John, 49
Harding, E. Y., 6
Harding, Edie, 78
Harding, Henry, 13, 14
Hare, W. C., 78
Harkley, John, 113
Harkness, John, 57, 73
Harola, Betsy, 104
Harold, Betsy, 106
Harp, Adolphus, 98
Harp, Charles, 77
Harp, Mary, 98
Harper, Henry, 89
Harper, William, 91
Harris, Ann Maria, 112
Harris, Ben, 2
Harris, G. G., 6
Harris, Hazel H., 87
Harris, Jesse H., 95
Harris, John H., 20
Harris, Rebecca, 98
Harris, Robert, 84, 114
Harris, Samuel, 102
Harris, Wesley, 85
Harrison, Daniel, 89
Harrison, Dennis, 35
Harrison, James, 109
Harrison, Joe, 88
Harrison, John A., 4
Harrison, Malinda, 42
Harrison, Mandred, 83
Harrison, Robert, 114
Harrison, Thomas, 102
Harrison, William, 1
Harrison, William H., 34
Hatton, Lethe, 80
Hautt, Edward, 17
Hawkins, William, 101
Hawkins, Charles, 32
Hawkins, Elijah, 114, 115
Hawkins, Evelina, 99
Hawkins, Fanny, 24
Hawkins, Frank, 88
Hawkins, Henson, 76
Hawkins, J. H., 18
Hawkins, James, 59, 93

Hawkins, Jim Henry, 82
Hawkins, John, 94
Hawkins, John F., 86
Hawkins, Nace, 95
Hawkins, Rachel, 99
Hawkins, Sam, 31
Hawkins, Sandy, 48
Hawkins, Thomas, 99
Hawley, Arianna, 50
Hayes, William, 98
Hays, William, 93
Hazell, W. C., 60
Hazzard, 16, 89
Helvins, Luke, 60
Hemsley, H., 1
Hemsley, Harriet, 1
Henderson, 23, 45, 66, 86
Henderson, Harriet, 66
Henderson, James, 23
Henderson, Mary, 86
Henny, Thomas, 26
Henrietta, 15, 19, 64, 78, 103
Henry, Charles, 27, 36, 80, 90
Henry, Francis, 105
Henry, George Patrick, 101
Henry, John, 8, 20, 36, 81, 88
Henry, Patrick, 86
Henry, William, 41, 113
Henson, 8, 12, 72, 76, 90, 93,
    103
Henson, Joe, 103
Henson, John, 72
Henson, Paul, 90
Herbert, 25, 39, 48, 81
Herbert, Charles, 25
Herbert, Solomon, 39
Herbert, William, 48
Hereford, John B., 50
Hickman, Albert, 51
Higgins, Harrison, 81
Higgins, John, 35, 47, 112
Hill, Alexander P., 19
Hill, Brian, 21
Hill, Charles, 20, 24, 25, 38, 70
Hill, Charles C., 50, 52
Hill, Clement, 62, 77
Hill, H. V., 8
Hill, Harry, 31

126

Hill, Henry, 46
Hill, Phillip, 90
Hill, Susan, 73
Hill, William, 99
Hill, William B., 49
Hill, William W., 33
Hillery, Nancy, 36
Hilton, 35
Hilton, John P., 35
Hines, Ben, 72
Hines, Jacob, 54
Hobbs, John, 112
Hobbs, Joseph, 113
Hodge, Nace, 46, 57
Hodges, Chloe, 4
Hodges, Lewis, 85
Holland, Henry, 63
Holland, John, 102
Holland, Mary, 78
Holliday, Susan, 58
Holliday, William F., 114
Holloday, James E. S., 110
Holmes, Harriet, 71
Holmes, Henrietta, 64
Holmes, Martha A., 64
Holmes, Mary A., 64
Holmes, Mrs., 4
Holmes, Patrick, 104
Hook, Birch, 78
Hooper, Martha, 114
Hooper, Peregrine, 114
Hoover, A., 4
Hoover, John, 35, 44
Hopewell, Harrison, 99
Hopkins, William, 74
Horne, E., 26
Horne, Edward, 13, 22, 26
Horner, Inman, 37
Horrick, Wilson, 98
Hoskinson, John R., 40
Howard, Caroline, 55
Howard, Dr. H. P., 38
Howard, H. P., 34
Howard, Jack, 77
Howard, James, 36, 115
Howard, Nancy, 24
Howard, Rebecca, 115
Howell, Susan G., 87

Hubbard, Henry, 16
Hughes, Robert Henry, 72
Hughes, William, 26
Humphreys, Harriet, 57
Humphreys, Walter, 51
Humpres, Margaret, 56
Hunt, George D., 93
Hunt, R. F., 36
Hunter, B. W. (Lt.), 9
Hunter, George H., 114
Hunter, George M., 29
Hunter, George, Jr., 20
Hunter, John H., 103
Hunter, Robert, 9
Hunter, William, 103
Hussy, William, 7
Hutton, Washington, 113
Hyatt, Seth, 12
Hynson, Sandy, 12
Iiggot, Mason, 80
Inglehart, 11, 107, 113
Inglehart, J. R., 11
Inglehart, Thomas J., 107
Iram. James, 55
Isaac, James C., 30
Isaacs, 30, 43, 92
Isaacs, Henry, 92
Isaacs, R. F., 43
Isaacs, John, 30
Jackson, Andrew, 61
Jackson, Ann, 37
Jackson, Asbury, 109
Jackson, B. J., 41
Jackson, Beverly, 2
Jackson, Charles, 27, 97
Jackson, E. H., 24
Jackson, Edward M., 81
Jackson, Emeline, 17
Jackson, Frank, 77
Jackson, Harriet, 109
Jackson, Henry, 21
Jackson, Isaac, 70, 71
Jackson, J. R., 23
Jackson, James, 9, 99
Jackson, John, 24, 63, 107,
111
Jackson, Mary, 50
Jackson, Patience, 76

Jackson, Phillip, 17
Jackson, Robert, 62
Jackson, Rufus, 25, 45, 75
Jackson, Sam, 70
Jackson, Samuel, 21, 95
Jackson, Sandy, 53
Jackson, Sarah, 22
Jackson, Thomas, 15, 16, 87
Jackson, Washington, 113
Jackson, William, 78, 79
Jacobs, Richard, 59
James Eliza, 69
James, Edward, 36
James, Henry, 92, 97
Jankins, R. E., 32
Javins, Thomas, 42
Jefferson, 44, 64, 69, 107
Jefferson, Thomas, 107
Jemmes, Alexander, 9
Jenifer, Jerry, 53
Jenkins, Charles, 77
Jenkins, J. Z., 27
Jenkins, John, 6
Jenkins, Joseph I., 10
Jenkins, thomas, 8
Jenkins, William, 103
Jennings, Jeremiah, 16
Jews, Jack, 33
Johnson, Robert, 28
John Henry, 8, 20, 36, 81, 88
John, Thomas, 25
Johns, Jane E., 53
Johnson, Agnes, 80
Johnson, Alexander, 24
Johnson, Amanda, 73
Johnson, Ann, 1, 4, 51
Johnson, Beverly, 19
Johnson, Bill, 111
Johnson, Bob, 35
Johnson, Charles, 22, 35, 66
Johnson, Dolly, 15
Johnson, Edward, 113
Johnson, Frank, 111
Johnson, George, 53, 85
Johnson, Henry, 13, 31, 60,
    61, 75, 88, 93
Johnson, Jacob, 111
Johnson, James, 40, 106

Johnson, Jemina, 22
Johnson, John, 59, 111
Johnson, John Barney, 67
Johnson, Josephine, 111
Johnson, Lewis, 111
Johnson, Louisa, 49, 59
Johnson, Lucy, 111
Johnson, Margaret, 54
Johnson, Martha, 79
Johnson, Mary, 37
Johnson, Nelly, 59
Johnson, Robert, 20, 35, 59
Johnson, Sally, 94
Johnson, William, 45, 54, 71,
    100
Johnston, William, 90
Jones Elizabeth, 74
Jones Harriet, 27
Jones, Albert, 56
Jones, Camille, 105
Jones, Catherine, 18
Jones, Charles, 55, 106
Jones, E. A., 32
Jones, Edward, 92
Jones, F. A., 22, 28
Jones, Henry, 57, 58
Jones, Isaac, 46
Jones, Jacob, 85
Jones, James, 15, 66
Jones, Joe, 113
Jones, John, 82, 89, 115
Jones, John C., 106
Jones, Lewis, 46
Jones, Mary, 14
Jones, Ned, 13
Jones, Nick, 115
Jones, Richard, 113
Jones, Sampson, 50
Jones, Tom, 66
Jones, William, 33, 69, 73, 77,
    113
Jones, William B., 11
Jopping, Caroline, 113
Kane, James H., 81
Keach, Alexander, 16
Keating, George, 86
Keech, A. Jr., 31

128

Lucas, Henry, 53
Lucas, Peter, 40
Lumby, Samuel, 29
Lusby, 16, 37, 61
Lyles, Alfred, 67, 103
Lyles, George, 93
Lyles, William, 25
Lynch, Henry, 28
Lynch, Sandy, 61
Lynham, W., 49
Lynn, Jinny, 106
Lyons, Charles, 96
Lyons, Jacob, 83
Lyons, William, 88
Mack, William, 18, 112
Mackall, 15, 27, 36, 43, 47, 65,
    78, 82, 83, 112
Mackall, B., 15, 78, 82
Mackall, Lewis, 27, 65, 83
Mackey, John H., 20
Mackey, Phillip, 62, 69
Mackill, Lewis, 31
Maddox, Catherine, 65
Magruder, E, 12, 30, 41
Magruder, Felder, 112
Magruder, J. B., 2
Magruder, John, 94
Magruder, Lloyd, 111
Maher, James, 45, 46
Mahoney, John, 68
Mahoney, Peyton, 34
Mallery, William H., 69
Mankins, James, 70
Mann, Allen, 85
Mann, John, 87, 101
Mann, R. A. B., 32
Manning, John, 101
Manning, William, 97
Marble, William, 65
Marbury, John H., 15
Marcellius, Daniael, 80
Marion, Francis, 70
Marklin, F., 22
Marlow, 18, 48, 85
Marlow, Henry, 48, 85
Marlowe, Catherine, 63
Marshall, Isaac, 42
Marshall, James, 1, 20

Marshall, James M., 60
Marshall, Josephus, 70
Marshall, Maria, 21
Marshall, Richard, 52
Marshall, Thomas, 36, 60, 65,
    108
Marshall, William, 68
Martin, Alfred, 5
Martin, C. D., 25, 26
Martin, Henry, 36
Martin, James P., 115
Martin, Pierce, 103
Martin, Thomas, 41
Martin, William, 15, 27, 39
Sewell, Priscilla, 24
Maryman, George, 1
Mason Romuel, 73
Mason, Eliza, 7
Mason, Lloyd, 47, 107
Mason, Romeo, 57
Mason, Thomas, 96
Massie, Thomas J., 44
Masters, Cerena, 11
Matener, Ben, 96
Mathews, H. C., 2
Mathias, Matthew, 93
Matthews, Alfred, 94
Matthews, Dennis, 84
Matthews, H. C., 23, 76, 83
Matthews, John, 12, 82, 98
Matthews, Lawrence, 75
Matthews, Resin, 99
Matthews, Samuel, 99
Mattingly, Benjamin, 100
Mattingly, Joseph H., 90, 94
Mattox, Milly
McBrown, Bill, 79
McCeney, Henry C., 49
McCormick, H., 41
McDermott, Michael, 18, 36,
    44
McGee, Robert, 109
McGill, R. T., 3
McGinis, James W., 13
McGruder, John H. G., 13
McLorten, J. A., 16
McPherson, John, 85
McSeeny, George, 101

Mead, Joseph, 48
Means, Lewis D., 66
Medley, John, 85
Merryman, H. R., 28, 67
Middleton, Charles S., 36
Middleton, Julia, 106
Milburn, Thomas, 77, 87
Milburn, Thomas H., 7
Miles, Joshua, 41
Miles, Lewis, 52
Mill, A. H., 21
Miller, Cornelius F., 114
Miller, J. B., 7
Miller, J. B., 7
Miller, Margaret A., 66
Miller, Matilda, 76
Miller, Thomas, 71
Miller, William, 103
Millis, Emily, 54
Mills, Ann, 54
Mills, Clark, 43
Mills, Clarke, 80
Mills, Emma, 77
Minor, Daniel, 37
Minor, J. R., 2, 3, 37
Minor, Mary, 27
Minor, P. H., 33
Missos, J. R., 3
Mitchell, George A., 28, 29
Mitchell, Henry, 106
Mitchell, John, 96, 113
Mitchell, L., 26
Mitchell, Mordecai, 44
Moken, James, 93
Monroe, F., 2
Montgomery, Albert, 98
Montgomery, George, 4
Moore, John, 95
Moore, William, 72
Moore, William M., 44
Morgan, E. E., 29
Morgan, George C., 58, 70
Morgan, William, 2, 3, 5, 6, 7, 8, 9
Morris, Lewis, 37
Morrison, William W., 18
Morsell, James S., 51
Mortimore, John, 37

Morton, Hon, J., 33
Morton, Jackson, 18, 23, 26
Morton, Maria F., 99
Morton, Strother, 84
Mosher, Theodore, 30, 78
Mosley, Aquila, 108
Mudd, Dominik., 4
Mudd, John W., 4
Muletta, George, 40
Mulligan, James, 47
Mulliken, Delli, 90
Mulliken, R. O., 14
Mullikin, John W., 23
Mulloy, 32, 45, 90, 91, 92
Muntz, Michael, 78
Murray, Henry G., 100, 106
Murray, Matthew H., 36
Murray, William, 39
Murrow, G. T., 22
Nailor, Allison, 8
Nansey, 9
Nat, 26, 108, 112
Naylor, Col. H., 38
Naylor, George, 88
Naylor, Henry, 65
Naylor, James, 1
Naylor, Judson, 50
Naylor, Robert, 88
Neal, Earnest, 11
Neal, John, 83
Neal, William B. T., 96
Neale, John E., 23
Nelson, Edwin, 86
Nelson, Jesse, 28
Nelson, John H., 4
Nelson, Phila, 74
Nelson, Richard F., 66
Nelson, William, 31
Nevitt, Robert K., 50
Newman, 38, 44, 51
Newman, G. W., 38, 44
Newman, George W., 51
Newman, John, 5
Newton, Harriet, 51
Newton, John, 21
Nicholls, William, 8
Nichols, Edward, 114
Nichols, Thomas, 79

Nikols, Abraham, 93
Nokes, James Jr., 29
Noland, William, 40
Norris, Andrew, 65
Norris, Joe, 78
Norton, Henry, 98
Norton, Rachel, 61
Noyes, John, 58, 70
Offet, Thomas M., 30
Offut, John, 41
Offut, William H., 111
Offut, William S., 41, 109
Ogle, Dick, 74
Ogle, Jerry, 69
Ogle, Moses, 96
Oliver, Charlotte, 109
Olliver, Richard, 100
Osborne, Lin, 1
Osbourne, 17, 33
Osbourne, J. A., 17
Osburn, Thomas H., 28, 29
Overhall, John, 2
Owens, James, 88
Padgett, Benjamin, 35, 112
Panay, Sarah, 33
Parker, Caroline, 48
Parker, George, 1, 43, 48, 56,
    87, 96, 100, 112
Parker, John, 56
Parkin, J. M., 2
Parr, Joseph, 101
Parsons, John, 13
Partes, Osea, 1
Pasco, Edward, 35
Patterson, Basil, 81
Patterson, Robert, 67
Paul, Edley, 67
Payne, Bill, 89
Payne, Savvannah, 35
Payton, John H., 6
Payton, John S., 16
Pecke, John, 12
Penn, Dr. H., 42
Penny, Isabella, 98
Perkins, 23, 43
Perkins, James T., 23
Perkins, Thomas, 43
Perris, Martha, 72

Perry, Benjamin, 76
Perry, Charles, 68
Perry, Elbert, 8
Perry, J. F., 28
Perry, James, 69
Perry, John, 63
Perry, William B., 107
Peters, George, 44, 91, 103
Peters, Richard Robert, 90
Peterson, John, 92
Petlow, John E., 5
Phillips, 15, 57, 61, 62, 73, 90
Phillips, George, 90
Phillips, Jerry, 57
Phillips, Sam, 15
Pierce, Jackson, 12
Pierce, William C., 93
Pinkney, Christina, 64
Pinney, Joseph, 20
Pirrer, Nancy, 100
Pirrer, Nathan, 100
Plater, Edward, 64
Pleasants, Sam, 59
Plummer, F. B., 26
Plummer, Henry, 89, 90
Plummer, John, 85
Plummer, John H., 79
Plummer, Sarah, 31
Poe, George Jr., 81
Pooley, George, 91
Porter, 25, 31, 95, 97, 98, 99,
    100, 101, 102, 103, 104,
    105, 106
Porter, Charles T., 25
Porter, H. W., 31
Posey, Alexander, 104
Posey, James, 96
Posey, William, 102
Powell, Jacob, 9
Powell, Thomas, 42
Prater, Patience, 75
Prater, Washington, 41
Prater, William, 66
Pratt, Samuel, 64
Price, C. W., 18
Price, Thomas, 23
Prim, Louisa, 10
Prine/Price, Dick, 108

Proter, A., 95, 97, 98, 99, 100, 101, 102, 103, 104, 105, 106
Pullison, Beverly, 100
Pumphery, William P., 41
Pumphrey, James B., 66
Pumphrey, Levi, 36, 47
Pumphrey, Samuel, 103
Pumphrey, William E., 13
Purdie, William H., 27
Queen, Henrietta, 78
Queen, Henry, 78
Queen, James, 8
Quigley, Frances, 16
Quigly, 18
R. H. Tunnell, 47
Randolph, John, 50
Ransels, Martin, 9
Raser, Ham, 98
Rawlings, David, 39
Reade, J. D., 22
Realey, Alexander, 94
Reaves, George, 93
Redab, Parker, 87
Redville, F., 13
Reed, George, 59
Reed, Michael, 30
Reed, Richard, 104
Reeder, William O., 107
Reynolds, William T., 103
Rhodes, George, 2
Rhodes, Mrs., 1
Richards, C. S., 30
Richards, Daniel, 89
Richards, George, 2, 15, 18, 24
Richards, George T, 7, 12, 25
Richards, George T., 5, 7, 12, 25
Richards, George T., 7
Richards, William, 8, 9, 11, 14, 15, 19
Richards, William H., 8, 11, 14, 15, 19
Richards, William H., 8
Richardson, 20, 37, 54, 62, 76, 91
Richardson, Bill, 76
Richardson, Justin, 20
Ricketts, Marchant, 66

Rideout, Lot, 87
Rigdon, Thomas, 94
Riggin, Thomas, 92
Riggs, Artemis, 115
Riggs, E., 39
Riley, Thomas, 61
Risin, James, 77
Rivers, Tilghman, 110
Roach/Rush, E. N., 22
Roberson, James, 31
Roberts, J. K., 16
Robertson, 11, 38, 72
Robertson, H. B., 4
Robey, E., 27, 28, 30, 49, 51, 52, 61, 65, 74, 75, 76, 79, 80, 81, 84, 86, 89
Robey, John E., 16, 27, 47, 49, 52, 53, 56, 57, 60, 67, 74
Robey, William, 25
Robinson, Etta, 53
Robinson, James, 54
Robinson, John, 83
Robinson, Matilda, 36
Robinson, Tom, 90
Robinson, William B., 60
Roden, Charles, 80
Rogers, Jack, 77
Rogers. Charles, 96
Rollins, David, 85
Rooison, M., 23
Ross, Ann, 80, 87
Ross, Fanny, 66
Ross, Jacob, 57
Ross, John, 112
Ross, Norman, 59
Ross, William R., 24
Ross, Henry D., 24
Ross, Ellen, 24
Rowles, E. C., 24
Rozier, Henry, 65
Rumsey, Edward, 33
Runner, John H., 65
Russell, 13, 48, 53
Russell, William H., 7
Ryan, Patrick, 69
Ryan, William, 79
Safborough, H., 6
Safes, Susannah, 5

Slater, David, 51
Slater, Thomas Henry, 56
Slater/Staten, 14
Slater/Staten, Jane, 14
Sly, Thomas B., 43
Smacum, Lewis Joseph, 43
Small, Jesse, 75, 76
Smallwood, Charles, 66
Smallwood, Henry, 96
Smallwood, Jacob, 86
Smallwood, Richard, 23
Smith, A., 6
Smith, Adam, 36, 97
Smith, Alan H., 27
Smith, Alfred, 111
Smith, Almira, 113
Smith, Arundel, 11
Smith, David, 68
Smith, Delia, 68
Smith, Elizabeth, 88
Smith, Emanuel, 82
Smith, Francis, 53
Smith, George, 97
Smith, George W., 92
Smith, Henry, 92, 103
Smith, James, 80, 98
Smith, James, Jane, 80, 98
Smith, James/Jane, 15
Smith, Jim, 91, 99
Smith, Joe, 84
Smith, John, 5, 19, 75, 92, 94, 96, 97, 106
Smith, John A., 24, 52, 101
Smith, Joseph, 104
Smith, Mary, 61, 84
Smith, Matilda, 69
Smith, Osborn, 70
Smith, R. N., 78
Smith, Samuel, 9
Smith, Sidney, 24
Smith, Thomas, 54
Smith, Washington, 36
Smith, William, 88, 95
Smoot, John, 100
Smoot, Margaret A. White, 110
Snowden, 10, 24, 47, 88, 91, 97
Snowden, Caleb, 24

Snowden, David, 91
Snowden, Isaac, 88
Snowden, John, 10
Snowden, Julia, 47
Snowden, Wesley, 97
Soden, Pierre, 40
Solomon, Alfred, 66
Soltleford, Thomas H., 6
Somby, Lucinda, 42
Somerville, James, 63
Sommers, James C., 34
Soper, Cloe Ann, 100
Soper, Nathaniel, 47
Southron, H., 41
Spaulding, B. O., 22
Spaulding, Joseph L., 77
Speake, Mary, 66
Speaks, Isiah, 95
Speaks, Joseph, 97
Spencer, William, 64
Spinks, James, 36, 45, 58, 59, 73
Sprigg, Billy, 2
Sprigg, Harriet, 111
Sprigg, John, 111
Sprigg, Orsben, 17
Sprigg, Samuel, 14
Sprigg, Solomon, 94
Sprigg, Thomas, 44, 58
Sprigg, William, 49
Spriggs, Thomas, 58
Spriggs/Spaggs, 22
Stafford, John G., 80
Stanmore, James, 51
Statley, Elizabeth, 83
Steel, william, 22
Stephens, Rezin, 29
Stepney, Charles, 6
Steuart, Frank, 77
Steuart, John, 76
Stevens, George, 113
Stevens, Reson, 30
Stevens, Samuel, 34
Stevenson, Chloe Ann, 21
Stevenson, Dick, 114
Stewart, Cealia, 13
Stewart, Eliza, 55
Stewart, Henry, 28, 34

Stewart, James, 1, 68
Stewart, John, 41, 68
Stewart, Samuel, 42
Stockett, Benjamin, 18
Stockett, William, 106
Stoddard, Charles, 93
Stokes, Daniel, 101
Stone, Phillip, 24
Stone, Thomas D., 18
Stone, William, 17, 42
Stonestreet, E., 22
Stonestreet, S. T., 20
Stover, Solomon, 43, 100
Strong, Samuel, 46
Strunser, John, 30
Stuart, Washington, 45
Suit, Edward, 95
Suit, John S., 19
Suit, O. B., 20
Suitte, Smith, 58
Sullivan, Charles, 96
Summers, 27, 32, 107
Summers, J. F., 27
Summers, John, 107
Summerville, Lewis, 59
Summerville, William H., 46
Susan, 7, 26, 27, 34, 39, 46,
   48, 50, 58, 71, 73, 87
Suttett, John, 22
Swain, Maria, 70
Swann, 50, 63, 106
Swann, Julia, 4
Swann, Thomas, 106
Swann, W. T., 50
Tabbs, Nace, 56
Tailor, Charles, 9
Talbot, William O., 74
Talbott, Thomas, 62
Tally, James, 50
Tarter, Robert T., 16
Tasker, Ben, 112
Tasker, Elias, 112
Tasker, John, 112
Tasker, Lewis, 112
Tasker, Ned, 112
Tasker, Virgie, 113
Taylor, Abraham, 93, 94
Taylor, Abram, 108

Taylor, B. O., 34
Taylor, Benjamin, 11, 25, 37
Taylor, Celia Ann, 37
Taylor, Clara, 76
Taylor, Elizabeth, 112
Taylor, George, 95
Taylor, Hariett A., 4
Taylor, Harriet, 4
Taylor, Isaac, 92
Taylor, John, 30
Taylor, Martha, 90
Taylor, Robert, 56
Taylor, William, 36, 47, 49
Taylor/Tyler, Alice, 11
Teale, Robert L., 44
Tell, William, 91
Thicker, James, 68
Thomas, Henry, 14, 46, 63
Thomas, Isaac, 11
Thomas, J. H., 108
Thomas, James, 6, 100
Thomas, Joe, 92
Thomas, John, 6, 12, 95
Thomas, John W., 10
Thomas, Levi, 89
Thomas, Mary Ann, 38
Thomas, Washington, 91
Thomas, William, 4, 42, 58
Thompson, Daniel, 99
Thompson, Eliza, 89
Thompson, George, 3, 23, 90,
   105
Thompson, Lewis, 45
Thompson, Lloyd, 55
Thompson, Richard, 55
Thompson, Smith, 3, 31
Thompson, Thomas, 100
Thorn, J. S., 3
Throckmorton, 20
Throckmorton, James, 20
Thurston, Tom, 69
Tiles, John H., 56
Tilghman, Richard, 44
Tilghman, Thomas, 38
Tilghman, William, 113
Till, William, 96
Tillman, Lewis, 37
Tinker, George, 3

Watkins, 14, 28, 38, 40, 70, 98, 114
Watkins, Dennis, 14
Watkins, Eliza, 28
Watkins, G. M., 38, 98
Watkins, George W., 114
Watkins, William M., 40
Watson, Bill, 78
Watson, Charles, 80
Watson, Edward, 34
Watson, Edwin, 28
Watson, Greenberg M., 30
Watson, John, 96
Watson, William, 3, 39
Watts, Charles, 88
Watts, Washington, 86, 108
Watts. Washington, 86, 108
Waugh, Mary E. D., 47
Weaver, Henry, 5
Weaver, John, 98
Weaver, Joseph, 65
Webb, Edgar, 62
Webb, William A., 94
Webster, 7, 11, 13, 32, 37
Webster, James G., 8
Webster, Ned, 32
Welch, Simon, 25
Welden Frank, 42
Weldon, Daniel, 50
Welsh, Aaron, 68
Wesley, Champoin, 57
Wesley, John, 62, 69, 71
West, Basil, 110, 111
West, Eliza A., 105
West, Hannah, 14
West, Henry, 72
West, Lloyd, 111
West, Samuel, 28
Wheeler, Alfred, 83
Wheeler, Peter, 108
Wheeler, Thomas, 24
Wheeler, Thomas C., 66
Whitaker, Moses, 84
White, Benjamin R., 110
White, Daniel, 98, 110
White, Daniel T., 90
White, Felis, 88
White, G., 27, 30

White, George, 46
White, Gustavius, 5
White, Gustavus, 43
White, H. A., 22
White, Henry, 94
White, Isaac, 46
Whiteman, Charles Goddard, 72
Wight, William, 112
Wight. O. C., 20
Wiley, Henry, 105
Wiley, John, 54
Wilkinson, 23
Williams, Billy, 30
Williams, Brooke, B., 34
Williams, Catherine, 54
Williams, Charles, 58, 82
Williams, Daniel, 108
Williams, Eliza, 6
Williams, Elizabeth, 24
Williams, Francis, 29
Williams, George, 40, 85
Williams, Grandville, 46
Williams, Harriet, 74
Williams, Henry, 53, 108
Williams, James, 11, 15, 61
Williams, Jasper Thomas, 109
Williams, John, 58
Williams, John H., 50
Williams, Lewellen, 55
Williams, Lucy, 10
Williams, Luke, 75
Williams, Ned, 83
Williams, Phillip, 83
Williams, Richard, 37, 79
Williams, Samuel W., 24
Williams, Sarah, 37
Williams, Stephen, 113
Williams, Thomas, 24, 93, 96
Williams, Toby, 37
Williams, William H., 1, 5, 6, 7, 8, 9, 10, 11, 12, 13, 15, 16
Williamson, Thomas, 93
Willison, William H., 6
Wills, Thomas, 34
Wilson, Benjamin, 30
Wilson, Clem, 35